AIRCRAFT
OF WORLD WAR II

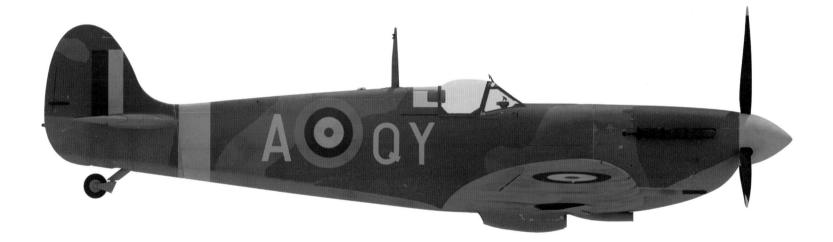

AIRCRAFT
OF WORLD WAR II

FEATURES SEVEN-VIEWS PER AIRCRAFT

ROBERT JACKSON

FALL RIVER PRESS

Editorial and design by
Amber Books Ltd

Project Editor: James Bennett
Designer: Brian Rust
Picture Research: Terry Forshaw

Artworks courtesy of Military Visualizations, Inc.

Fall River Press
122 Fifth Avenue
New York, NY 10011

ISBN: 978-1-4351-1440-1

Printed and bound in China

1   3   5   7   9   10   8   6   4   2

Contents

Introduction

Between 1939 and 1943, huge advances were made in the capability of combat aircraft. From Britain came the legendary Spitfire and Hurricane, and the bombers that would take the war to the heart of Germany: the Wellington and Lancaster, while from the United States came the B-17 Flying Fortress, the B-24 Liberator, and the fighters that would enable the American daylight bombers to survive during their early forays into hostile skies: the P-47 Thunderbolt and the P-38 Lightning. With these aircraft, Allied forces would pound the Third Reich around the clock, the RAF by night and the USAAF by day.

BOEING B-17G FLYING FORTRESS

FOCKE-WULF FW 190D

In North Africa, decisive battles were being fought, culminating in the last stand of the Axis forces in Tunisia early in 1943. Aircraft such as the Messerschmitt Bf 110, already defeated by the Spitfire and Hurricane in the Battle of Britain, now found itself at the mercy of Allied fighters like the Curtiss P-40 Warhawk, flown by capable British, Austalian, South African and American pilots. Elsewhere, on the great plains of Russia, a combination of winter weather and bitter Soviet resistance had brought the triumphant German offensives to a standstill. The Soviet aviation industry was now beginning to produce excellent combat aircraft in huge numbers; types like the Yakovlev Yak-3, arguably the most manoeuvrable fighter to see combat in World War II and which went on to provide the basis for Russia's first jet fighter. Aircraft such as this could at last counter Germany's formidable Focke-Wulf Fw 190, the 'Butcher Bird' that was at least the equal of Allied fighter types in the west, and better than most.

But it was in the west that the decisive air battles were fought. Now, at last, the Allies had a fighter – the North American P-51 Mustang – that could escort the bombers of the USAAF all the way to Berlin and back, and face the sternest challenge of the last months of the war – the Messerschmitt Me 262 jet fighter, deployed in increasing numbers from the autumn of 1944. The Me 262 was the shape of future conflict in the air, and its aerodynamic design would be reflected in the jet-powered combat aircraft of east and west that would appear in the early post-war years. There were other radical innovations, too: amazing aircraft like the rocket-powered Me 163, as much a danger to its pilots as to the enemy, which laid the foundation for much high-speed rocket research after the war.

MESSERSCHMITT ME 262

Finally, on the other side of the world, the aircraft that had helped to forge many of Japan's early victories, the Mitsubishi Zero, had at last met its match in the shape of the nimble Grumman Hellcat naval fighter, which destroyed more enemy aircraft than any other in World War II, and played an enormous part in securing final victory for the Allies. But it was the Boeing B-29 Superfortress, the most advanced piston-engined bomber of all, that delivered the killing blows at Hiroshima and Nagasaki.

MITSUBISHI A6M2 ZERO

Creating the Digital Models

Every aircraft in this book was originally created as a complex 3D object using computer graphics software commonly employed in the production of movies and video games. From the 3D model, each of the seven-view images was generated, or rendered, from various viewpoints (above, below, etc) around the model. The result is a set of highly detailed 2D images suitable for printing.

1 All 3D objects start with a single point, called a vertex. Its position in the virtual 'space' in the graphics program can be defined by three parameters: X, Y and Z or, in more basic terms, left and right, up and down and back and forth.

2 Once you have three vertices, they can be joined to form a 2D triangle in 3D space, called an edged face.

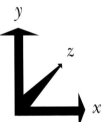

3 This is the starting point for creating an aircraft wheel. Every point along this outline is a vertex defined by different values for X and Y. It forms a 2D shape in 2D space. At the moment it does not exist in three dimensions. As you can see, it is a cross-section through half of the wheel, from the tyre treads at the bottom to the axle at the top.

4 Using complex mathematics, the computer graphics program 'lathes' the 2D shape in the Z axis, drawing a wheel shape in three dimensions around the axle, which is on the X axis.

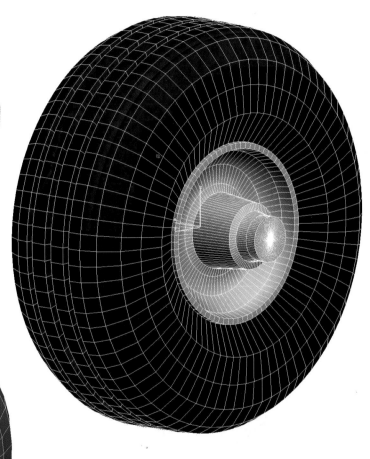

5 The end result is a 3D wheel. Although it appears solid, it is composed of hundreds of edged faces, themselves made up of lines and vertices.

6 Although the wheel now looks solid, it needs texture and lighting to make it look 'real'.

7 A texture is applied to the finished wheel to give the appearance of pitted rubber and aluminium. Texture is applied by wrapping a stored 2D texture around a 3D object.

8 The texture contains the information about how the object will appear in different lights and different angles. A texture must be created for every element on the aircraft.

9 To create more complex objects, simple elements are fitted together to form an assembly like this undercarriage unit.

10 The finished 3D undercarriage unit can be textured, painted and lit. Finally it can be rendered from any angle.

Avro Lancaster

One of the most effective bomber aircraft of World War II, and famous for its attack on the Ruhr dams in 1943, the Avro Lancaster was developed from the Avro Manchester, a design that suffered from the unreliability of its two Rolls-Royce Vulture engines. While Manchester production was in progress, one airframe was fitted with four Rolls-Royce Merlin XX engines. This prototype Lancaster first flew on 9 January 1941. The first operational Lancaster was delivered to the Royal Air Force's No. 44 (Rhodesia) Squadron at Waddington, Lincolnshire, in September 1941 for familiarization. By January 1942, the squadron had begun to replace its Handley Page Hampdens with the type. At peak strength in August 1944, Lancasters armed no fewer than 42 Bomber Command squadrons. They remained in service for some time after World War II. RAF Coastal Command used the GR.3 maritime patrol version.

- The first operational sortie with Lancasters took place on 3 March 1942, when four RAF aircraft laid mines in the Heligoland Bight.
- The last Lancaster raid of World War II was against an SS barracks at Berchtesgaden on 25 April 1945.
- During the war, Lancasters flew 156,192 sorties, dropping 608,612 tons of bombs. Losses in action were 3431 aircraft, with a further 246 being destroyed in operational accidents.

SPECIFICATIONS

TYPE: *Seven-seat heavy bomber*

POWERPLANT: *Four 1223 kW (1,750 hp) Merlin 24 inverted inline piston engines*

PERFORMANCE: *Maximum speed: 462 km/h (286 mph) at 3500 m (11,480 ft); Range: 2700 km (1,674 miles) with 6350 kg (13,970 lb) bombload; Service ceiling: 7467 m (24,492 ft)*

WEIGHTS: *Empty: 16,783 kg (36,923 lb); loaded 30,845 kg (67,859 lb)*

ARMAMENT: *Nine 7.7 mm (.303 cal.) Browning machine guns plus up to 6350 kg (14,000 lb) of bombs*

DIMENSIONS: *Span: 31.09 m (102 ft); Length: 21.18 m (69 ft); Height: 6.25 m (20 ft); Wing area: 120.49 m² (1,296 sq ft)*

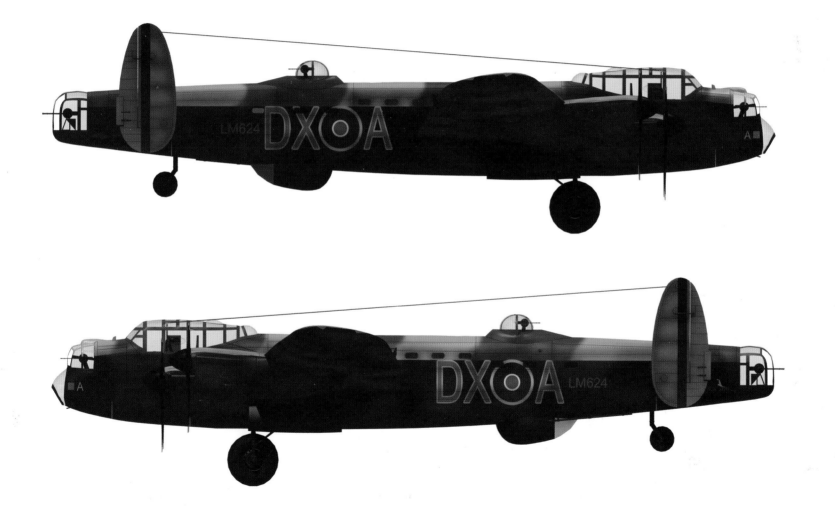

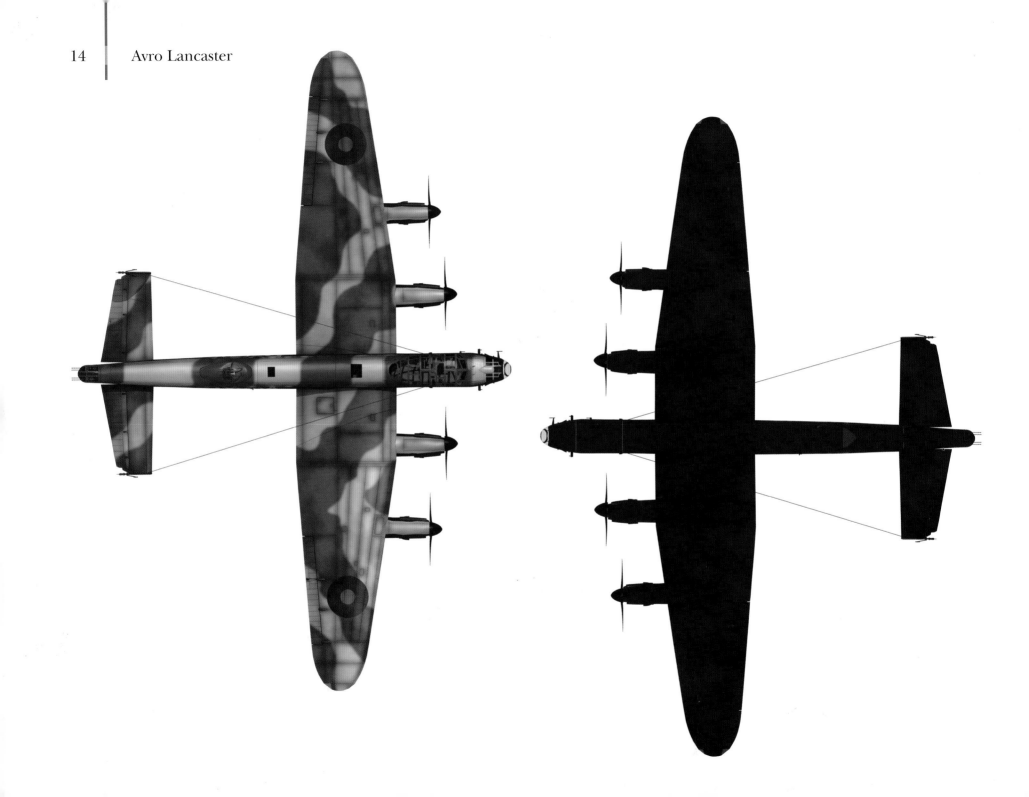

No. 57 Squadron
Lancaster Mk III DX-A belonged to No. 57 Squadron, RAF Bomber Command, which flew Lancasters successively from Methwold in Norfolk, Scampton and East Kirby in Lincolnshire. Before rearming with Lancasters, the squadron operated first with Blenheims, then Wellingtons, during World War II.

COSTLY RAIDS

The RAF Battle of Britain Memorial Flight's Avro Lancaster Mk I is pictured here in the markings of No 44 (Rhodesia) Squadron. In April 1942, this unit carried out a famous – and costly – daylight mission to Augsburg in Bavaria to attack a factory making parts for U-boat engines. Of all the thousands of Lancasters built, only two remain in an airworthy condition.

Boeing B-17 Flying Fortress

One of the most famous combat aircraft of all time, the Boeing B-17 Flying Fortress was the backbone of the US daylight bombing offensive against Germany in World War II, carrying out precision attacks against targets deep inside enemy territory from bases in England and Italy. During its early operations, it suffered terrible losses, disproving the theory that heavily armed bombers could operate in enemy skies without fighter escort. It was not until the long-range North American Mustang fighter became available early in 1944 that matters improved. The B-17 was particularly vulnerable to head-on fighter attack, and the B-17G version was fitted with a power-operated chin turret armed with two 12.7 mm (0.50 in) machine guns. This gave the B-17G, the major production model, a total of 13 heavy machine guns.

- The first B-17G was delivered on 4 September 1943 and the last on 13 April 1945, less than a month before the German surrender.
- B-17Gs were used by the RAF in the electronic countermeasures (ECM) role
- Three B-17Gs were acquired by the new State of Israel in 1948, and ferried from the United States via Panama, Portugal and Czechoslovakia. They were used operationally during the 1948–49 War of Independence, one of them carrying out an attack on Cairo airport.

SPECIFICATIONS

TYPE: *Long-range bomber*

POWERPLANT: *Four 895 kW (1,200 hp) Wright R-1820-97 Cyclone turbocharged radial piston engines*

PERFORMANCE: *Maximum speed: 462 km/h (287 mph) at 7690 m (25,230 ft); Range: 3220 km (2000 miles) with 2725 kg (6,007 lb) load*

WEIGHTS: *Empty: 16,391 kg (36,136 lb); Loaded 29,710 kg (65,499 lb)*

ARMAMENT: *Thirteen 12.7 mm (.50 cal.) machine guns in twin turrets, plus single dorsal and fore and aft beam positions; 8000 kg (1,7640 lb) maximum bombload*

DIMENSIONS: *Span: 31.62 m (103 ft 9 in); Length: 22.66 m (74 ft 4 in); Height: 5.82 m (19 ft 1 in); Wing area: 131.92 m² (1,420 sq ft)*

BOEING B-17G FLYING FORTRESS

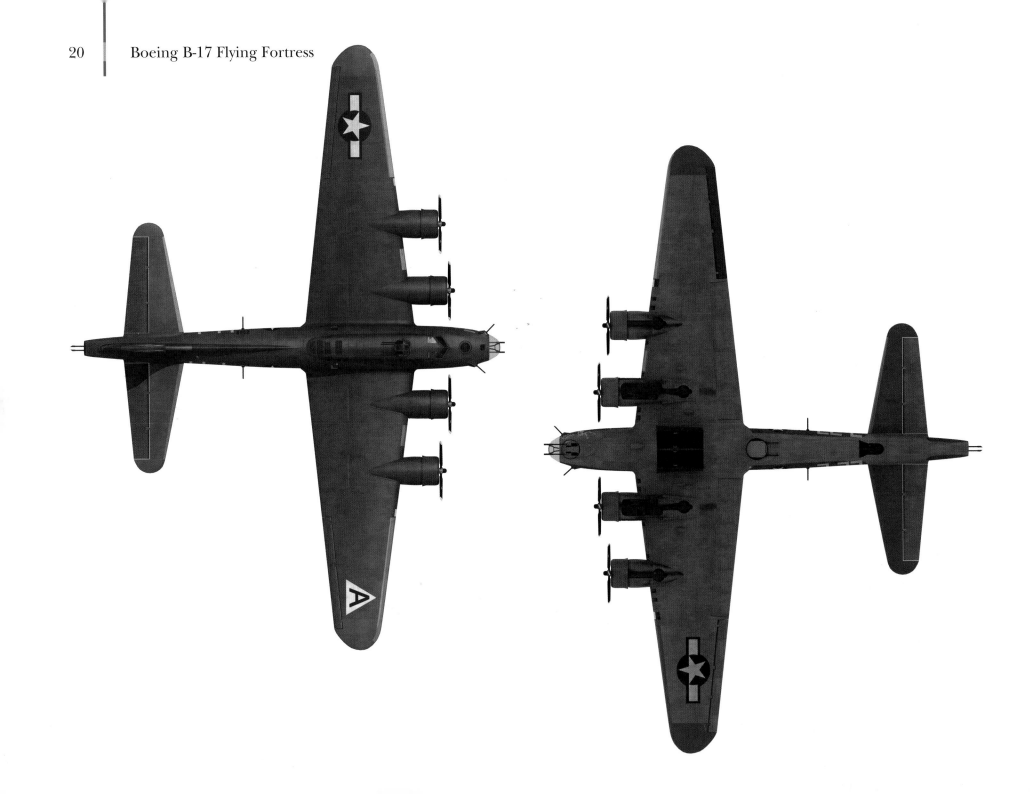

The 'Ragged Irregulars'

Pictured here is a Boeing B-17G Flying Fortress of the 401st Bomb Squadron, Eighth Air Force, US Army Air Forces. Based in Bassingbourn, Cambridgeshire, in 1942–45, the 401st Bomb Squadron was one of four squadrons belonging to the 91st Bomb Group, the 'Ragged Irregulars'.

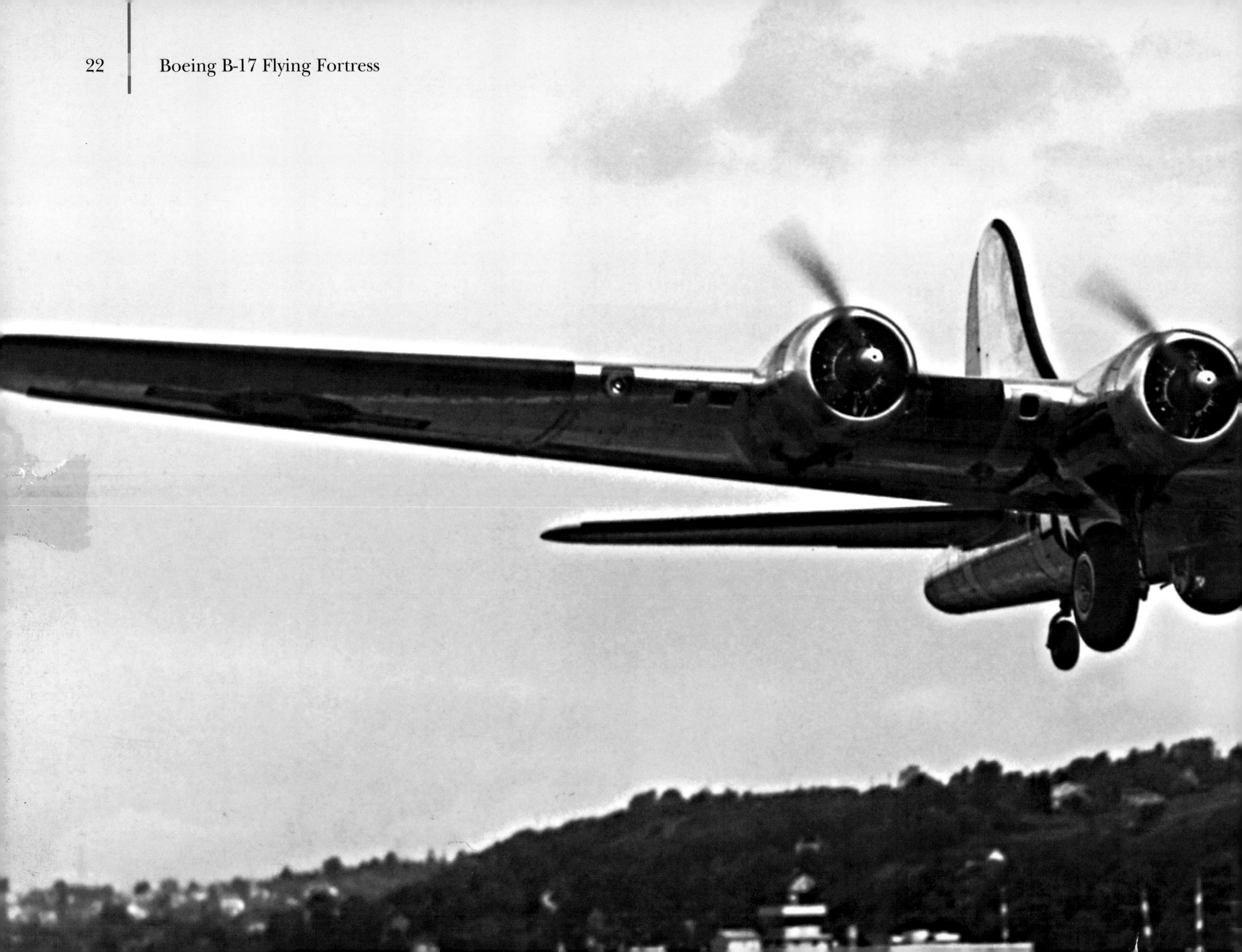

CREW VULNERABILITY

The B-17 was a complex piece of machinery designed to deliver bombs from high altitude over long ranges. By the last year of World War II, it was bristling with machine guns to fend off enemy fighter attacks. It was not a comfortable environment for its crew during the lengthy missions they had to fly. The two most vulnerable crew members were the tail gunner and ball turret gunner. The tail gunner operated his twin 12.7 mm (0.50 in) machine guns while kneeling on special pads, and if he was wounded it was almost impossible to reach him. It was equally difficult to extricate the ball turret gunner, sealed inside his position under the fuselage, defending the bomber against attacks from below.

Boeing B-29 Superfortress

Famous as the heavy bomber that brought strategic air warfare to the Japanese home islands during the last year of the Pacific war, and above all as the aircraft that carried out the nuclear attacks on Hiroshima and Nagasaki, the Boeing B-29 Superfortress was the outcome of design studies begun in 1937. The definitive design met a 1940 US Army Air Corps requirement for an aircraft capable of carrying 907 kg (2,000 lb) of bombs for 8582 km (5,333 miles) at 644 km/h (400 mph). The first XB-29 prototype flew on 21 September 1942. The first units to be equipped with the B-29 were deployed to bases in India and Southwest China in the spring of 1944. The establishment of five operational bases in the Marianas in March 1944 brought the B-29s much closer to Japan, and five bombardment wings were quickly redeployed there.

- Early high-altitude missions had poor results, mainly because of adverse weather conditions in target areas, but also because the B-29's technical complexity resulted in a high rate of equipment failures.
- The B-29's move to the Marianas was followed by a complete revision of tactics, the B-29s now carrying out large-scale night incendiary area attacks on Japan's principal cities, with devastating results.
- The B-29s that dropped the atomic bombs on Hiroshima and Nagasaki on 6 and 9 August 1945, 'Enola Gay' and 'Bock's Car', belonged to the 509th Bombardment Wing (Provisional), which was to become the principal US nuclear weapons trials unit.

SPECIFICATIONS

TYPE: *Long-range strategic bomber*

POWERPLANT: *Four 1641 kW (2,200 hp) Wright R-3350 Cyclone 18 turbocharged radial piston engines*

PERFORMANCE: *Maximum speed: 576 km/h (358 mph); Range: 5230 km (3,250 miles); Service ceiling: 9170 m (30,085 ft)*

WEIGHTS: *Empty: 31,815 kg (70,140 lb); loaded 56,245 kg (123,999 lb)*

ARMAMENT: *Two 12.7 mm (.50 cal.) machine guns in each of four remotely-controlled turrets and three 12.7 mm guns or two 12.7 mm guns and one 20 mm (0.79 in) cannon in the tail; bombload 9072 kg (20,000 lb)*

DIMENSIONS: *Span: 43.05 m (141 ft 3 in); Length: 30.18 m (99 ft 2 in); Height: 9.02 m (29 ft 7 in); Wing area: 161.27 m² (1,736 sq ft)*

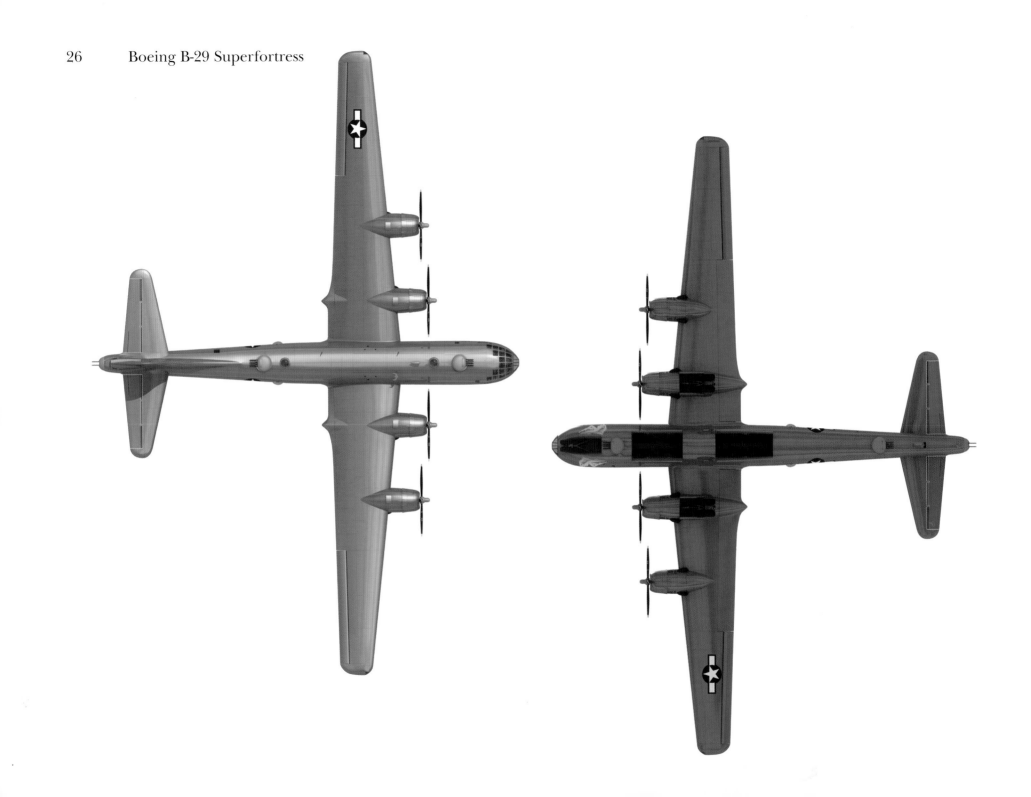

Pacific Bombing Veteran
B-29 'Lucky Lady' of the 504th Bombardment Group was a veteran of many bombing missions over Japan, as the mission symbols just behind the cockpit testify. The 504th BG also carried out mining operations.

PROUD CAREER

This aircraft, named 'Eddie Allen' after the Boeing test-pilot killed when the B-29 prototype crashed in February 1943, is pictured on its first operational deployment in the Pacific. The B-29 continued to be the mainstay of the US Air Force's Strategic Air Command for several years after 1945, and the aircraft saw almost continual action during the three years of the Korean War. The first B-29 strike of that conflict was carried out by the Guam-based bombers of the 20th Air Force's 19th Bombardment Wing on 13 July 1950, and the offensive was maintained against North Korean troop concentrations, communications and industrial targets throughout August, September and October. During that period, the B-29s dropped more than 30,480 tonnes (30,000 tons) of bombs on North Korean targets, surpassing the total dropped on Japan during World War II.

Bristol Beaufighter

The heavily armed twin-engined Bristol Beaufighter, equipped with airborne interception (AI) radar, gave the Royal Air Force its first effective means of defence against enemy night bombers. The first AI-assisted Beaufighter kill was claimed on the night of 19/20 November 1940, when Flt Lt John Cunningham and Sgt Phillipson of No. 604 Squadron were credited with destruction of a Junkers 88. The Beaufighter was also developed into a highly effective anti-shipping aircraft, armed with bombs or torpedoes. Initially, many were lost in accidents as a result of stalling on the landing approach. The aircraft's increasingly fearsome reputation among aircrew was dispelled when one made a perfect approach and touchdown at an RAF station, and its pilot proved to be a very glamorous young lady of the Air Transport Auxiliary.

- On 10 May 1941, the last major Luftwaffe attack on London, Beaufighters destroyed 14 German bombers, the Luftwaffe's highest loss on any one night since it began its night offensive against the British Isles.
- Beaufighters were used in North Africa in the ground-attack role, in the Far East and in the Pacific, where they were operated by the Royal Australian Air Force.
- The Beaufighter TFX – the torpedo-carrying version – was the most important British anti-shipping strike aircraft until the end of the war.

SPECIFICATIONS

TYPE: *Two-seat low-level strike fighter*

POWERPLANT: *Two 1320 kW (1,770 hp) Bristol Hercules XVIII radial piston engines*

PERFORMANCE: *Maximum speed: 488 km/h (330 mph) at 400 m (1,312 ft); Range: 2366 km (1,470 miles); Service ceiling: 4570 m (29,000 ft)*

WEIGHTS: *Empty: 7076 kg (15,507 lb); loaded 11,431 kg (25,200 lb)*

ARMAMENT: *Six forward-firing 7.7 mm (.303 cal.) machine guns and one flexible 7.7 mm Vickers 'K' machine gun in dorsal position; four forward-firing 20 mm (0.79 in) cannon, plus one torpedo and two 113 kg (230 lb) bombs or eight 41 kg (90 lb) air-to-surface rockets*

DIMENSIONS: *Span: 17.63 m (58 ft) Length: 12.70 m (42 ft); Height: 4.83 m (16 ft); Wing area: 46.73 m² (503 sq ft)*

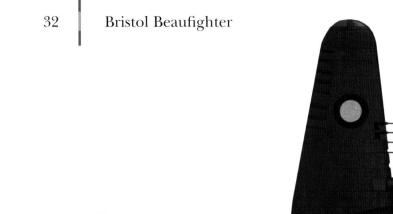

Pacific Duty
A Bristol Beaufighter Mk.21 of No. 31 Squadron, Royal Australian Air Force. The squadron's ground-attack Beaufighters destroyed 54 Japanese aircraft and nine ships by the end of the Pacific war.

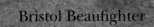

FEARFUL ARMAMENT

Apart from its AI radar, the Beaufighter's main asset was its very heavy armament of four cannon and six machine guns, which could literally tear an enemy bomber apart. The torpedo-carrying version, known as the Torbeau, carried an additional machine gun under a dorsal cupola. This variant usually had a crew of two, but there was space for a third crew member behind the pilot, his task being to help aim the torpedo. The 45.7 cm (18 in) torpedo carried by the Torbeau was fitted with a Mono Air Tail (MAT), which stabilized the torpedo after it was dropped. The MAT was released upon impact with the water. Coastal Command Beaufighters often carried ASV (Air to Surface Vessel) radar to locate shipping targets.

Consolidated B-24 Liberator

The B-24 Liberator was notable for its long range, which made it ideal for operations in the Pacific and for attacks on targets in the Balkans from bases in North Africa. Built in larger numbers than any other US warplane of World War II (18,431 were produced in total), the Liberator was delivered in greater quantities than any other bomber in aviation history. The B-24 made its operational debut in June 1942 with long-range raids from Egypt against the Romanian oilfields. In the Pacific, although the Boeing B-29 prosecuted the strategic air offensive against the Japanese home islands, it was the Liberator that remained the principal strategic bomber elsewhere in the theatre. The RAF also made extensive use of the aircraft, mainly in Southeast Asia, where it equipped 14 squadrons, and its maritime reconnaissance counterpart closed the 'mid-Atlantic gap' where air cover for the vital Atlantic convoys had previously been absent.

- The B-24 was easily recognized by its distinctive twin tail fins and the long, high aspect ratio wing.
- Its fuselage was very deep, to accommodate the required bomb load; to facilitate ground handling and produce shorter take-off runs a tricycle undercarriage with a steerable nosewheel was adopted.
- The deep fuselage of the B-24 was less streamlined than that of the B-17 Flying Fortress, and the Liberator tended to burn more easily when seriously hit.

SPECIFICATIONS

Type: *Heavy bomber*

Powerplant: *Four 895 kW (1,200 hp) Pratt & Whitney R-1830-43 Twin Wasp radial piston engines*

Performance: *Maximum speed: 488 km/h (300 mph); Range: 2896 km (2,850 miles); Service ceiling: 9900 m (32,500 ft)*

Weights: *Empty: 15,413 kg (34,000 lb); Maximum take-off: 27,216 kg (60,000 lb)*

Armament: *one 12.7 mm (.50 cal.) nose gun (some with additional 12.7 mm fixed nose guns), two more each in dorsal turret, tail turret, retractable ball turret, and waist positions, plus maximum internal bombload of 3629 kg (8,800 lb)*

Dimensions: *Span: 33.52 m (110 ft); Length: 20.22 m (66 ft 4 in); Height: 5.46 m (17 ft 11 in); Wing area: 97.36 m² (1,048 sq ft)*

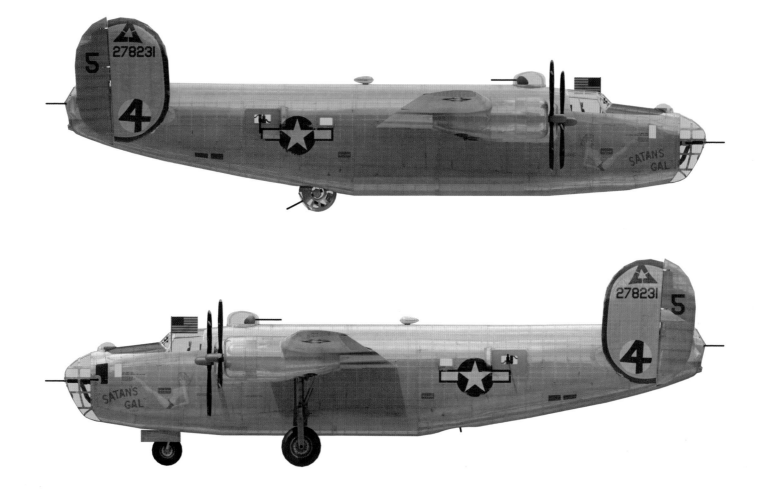

Strategic Bombing
B-24J 'Satan's Gal' was operated by the 720th Bombardment Squadron of the 450th Bombardment Group, a Fifteenth Air Force formation that began operations in Italy in January 1944. It was deactivated on 15 October 1945.

VALOUR IN COMBAT

The B-24 could absorb a huge amount of battle damage and still remain airborne. On 16 June 1943, for example, a B-24 of the 43rd Bombardment Group was carrying out a photo-mapping mission over the Solomon Islands in the Pacific when it was attacked by 20 Japanese fighters. Although seriously wounded, the bombardier, 2nd Lt Joseph R. Sarnoski, remained at the nose gun position and continued firing at the enemy until he died at his post; the pilot, Captain Jay Zeamer, Jr, continued to take evasive action despite being severely injured, then directed the aircraft to a base more than 800 km (500 miles) away. Both men were awarded the Medal of Honor. Shown here is a B-24J of the 577th Bombardment Group, USAF, landing at RAF Valley in Anglesey, Wales.

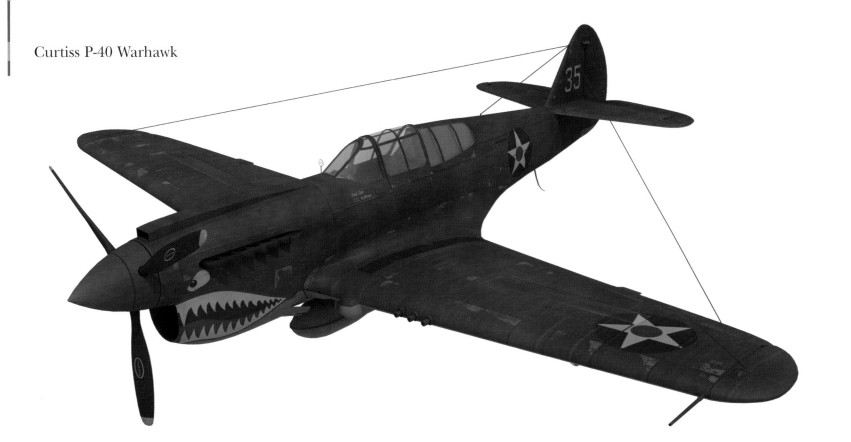

Curtiss P-40 Warhawk

Although never an outstanding combat aircraft, the Curtiss P-40 served in every theatre of war. Moreover, it was available in quantity at a critical period of World War II, when more advanced combat aircraft were still at the testing stage. The fighter was famously flown by the American Volunteer Group, the 'Flying Tigers', which began operations in December 1941 from Kunming, China, and Mingaladon, Burma, in defence of the Burma Road and the Sino-Burmese border. But the P-40 was no match for aircraft such as the Messerschmitt Bf 109F or the Japanese Zero fighter. Compared with contemporary fighters such as the Spitfire, it was a heavy aircraft. Its high diving speed was an advantage for ground-attack work, but it performed poorly in air combat. Although considered unsuitable for operational use by Fighter Command, the P-40s were used in the tactical reconnaissance role. P-40s were also supplied to the Soviet Union.

- The P-40 performed sterling work in the tactical support role in the Western Desert, serving with the RAF's Desert Air Force, in which it was also operated by Australian and South African squadrons.
- P-40s saw action in the defence of the Hawaiian Islands, the Philippines, Australia and New Guinea.
- Many of the P-40s used by the RAF were originally destined for the French air force, but France was overrun before they could be delivered.

SPECIFICATIONS

TYPE: *Single-seat interceptor and fighter-bomber*

POWERPLANT: *One 1015 kW (1,360 hp) Allison V-1710-81 inline piston engine*

PERFORMANCE: *Maximum speed: 609 km/h (378 mph) at 3210 m (10,530 ft); Range: 386 km (240 miles); Service ceiling: 11,630 m (38,160 ft)*

WEIGHTS: *Empty: 2724 kg (6,045 lb); Loaded: 4018 kg (8,858 lb)*

ARMAMENT: *Six 12.7 mm (.50 cal.) machine guns in wing; provision for 227 kg (500 lb) bomb or 197 litre (52 gallon) drop-tank under fuselage*

DIMENSIONS: *Span: 11.42 m (37 ft 6 in); Length: 10.20 m (33 ft 6 in); Height: 3.77 m (12 ft 4 in); Wing area: 21.95 m² (236 sq ft)*

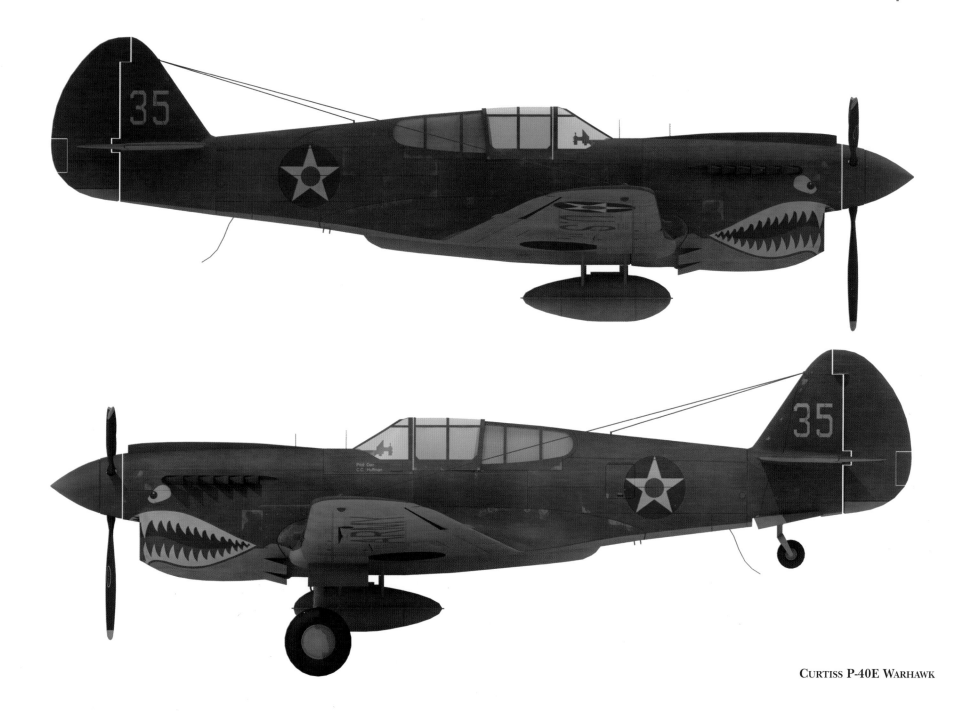

CURTISS P-40E WARHAWK

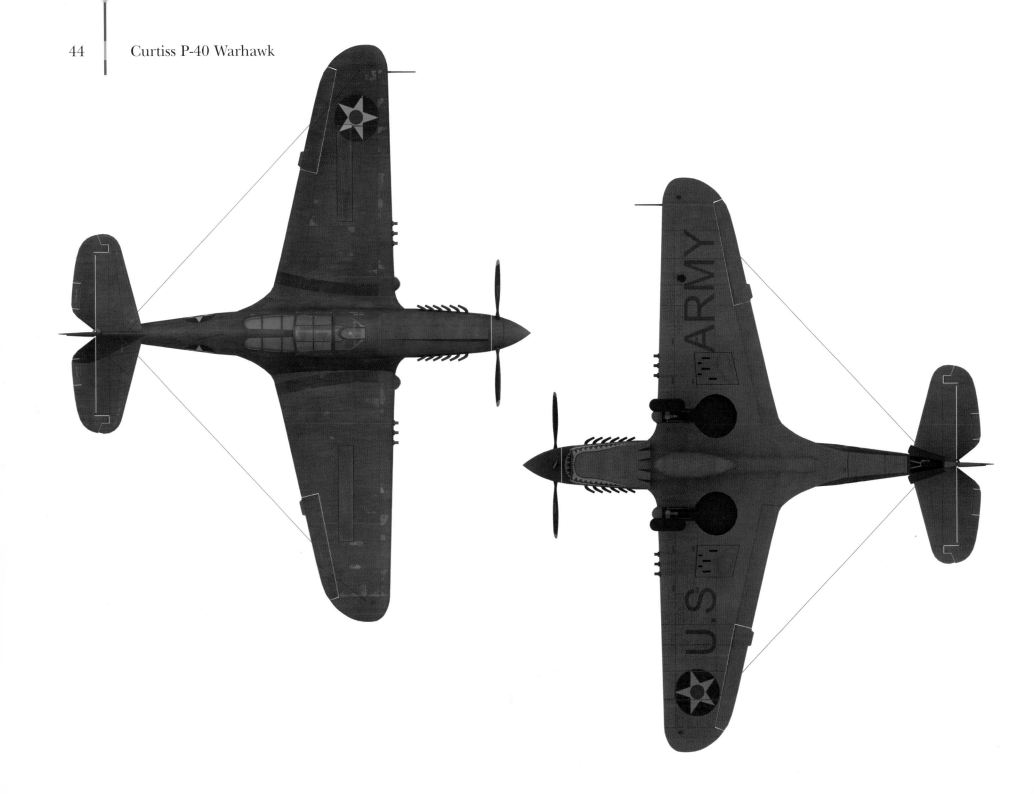

The 'Flying Tigers'
A Curtiss P-40E of the American Volunteer Group, the famous 'Flying Tigers'. The AVG put up a gallant resistance against the Japanese in China and Burma, and eventually became the cornerstone of the US Fourteenth Air Force.

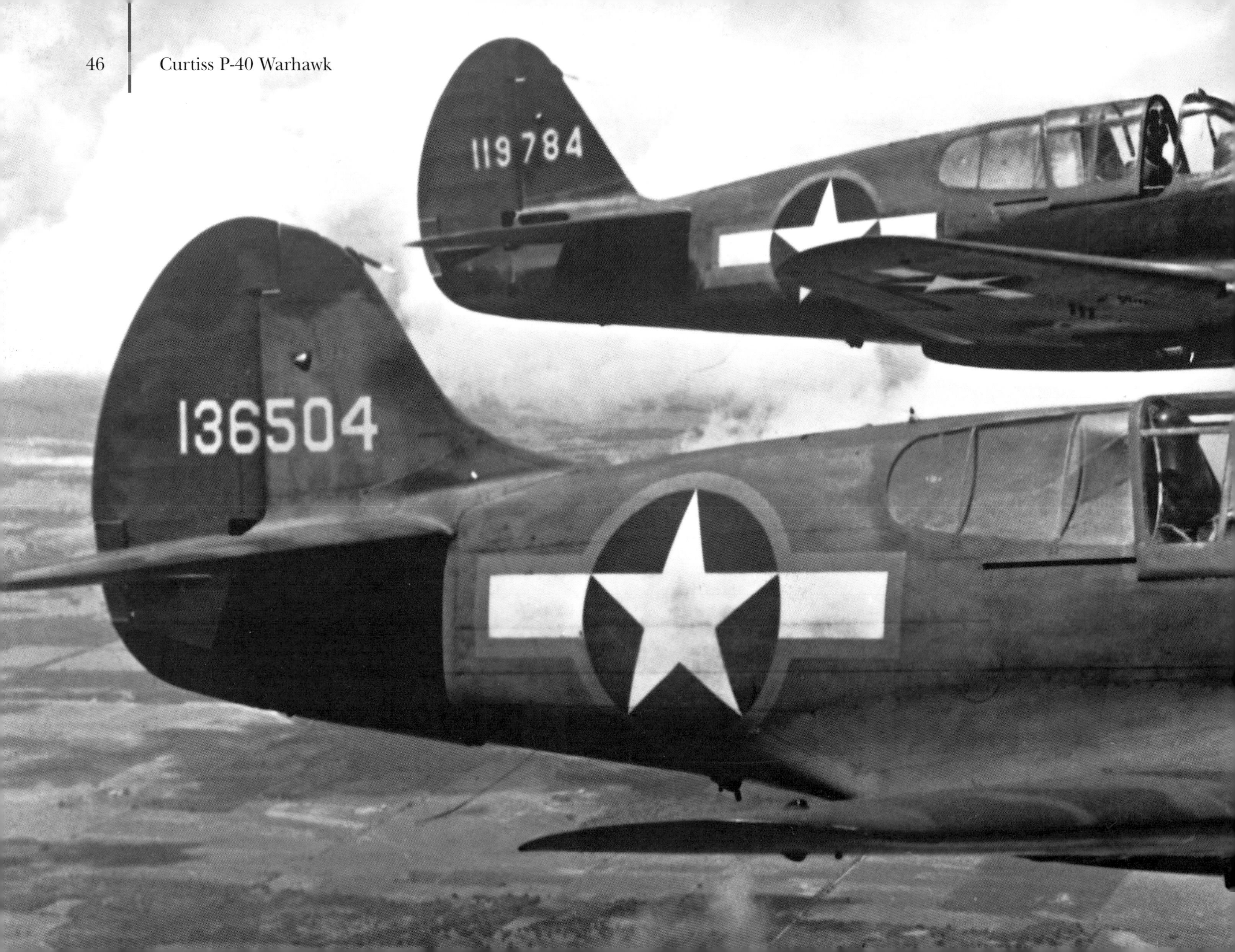
119784
136504

STURDY CONSTRUCTION

While visibility from the P-40 Warhawk's cockpit was poor, it was adequate for the aircraft's primary role of ground attack. The aircraft's Allison engine also performed well at low altitude. The inlet duct above the engine allowed air into the carburettor, which was situated at the rear of the engine. The large chin air intake of the P-40 admitted cooling air for three radiators; the central radiator was for the oil, whereas the two outer radiators cooled the glycol engine coolant. The P-40 was a strong aircraft and could absorb a considerable amount of damage, a useful attribute in the ground-attack role. Pictured are a pair of P-40E Warhawks on a training flight.

de Havilland Mosquito

The de Havilland DH.98 Mosquito was one of the most versatile and successful aircraft of World War II. It saw service as a day and night fighter, fighter-bomber, high altitude bomber, pathfinder, anti-shipping strike aircraft, reconnaissance aircraft and trainer. The photo-reconnaissance variant was the first into service, being issued to the No. 1 Photographic Reconnaissance Unit at RAF Benson, Oxfordshire, in September 1941. The first Mosquito B.IV bombers went to No. 105 Squadron at Marham, Norfolk, in May 1942. The major production version of the Mosquito was the FB.Mk.VI, which entered service in the spring of 1943 and subsequently armed several squadrons of the Royal Air Force's No. 2 Group.

- Conceived in 1938, the Mosquito was an all-wood construction; this produced a relatively light aircraft with a high speed, and it also alleviated the problem of strategic metals shortages in time of war.
- B.IV bombers made their first operational sortie on 31 May 1942. Five aircraft were sent to Cologne to photograph damage caused by the previous night's 1000-bomber raid and to drop a few bombs.
- No. 2 Group squadrons carried out some daring low-level precision attacks during the last year of the war, including the raid on Amiens prison in February 1944 and attacks on Gestapo headquarters buildings in Norway and the Low Countries.

SPECIFICATIONS

TYPE: *High-speed light bomber*

POWERPLANT: *Two 918 kW (1,230 hp) Rolls-Royce Merlin 21 inline piston engines*

PERFORMANCE: *Maximum speed: 612 km/h (379 mph) at 6400 m (21,000 ft); Range: 3000 km (1,860 miles); Service ceiling: 10,500 m (34,450 ft)*

WEIGHTS: *Empty: 6400 kg (14,080 lb); loaded 10,200 kg (22,440 lb)*

ARMAMENT: *Four 227 kg (500 lb) bombs*

DIMENSIONS: *Span: 16.51 m (54 ft); Length: 12.43 m (41 ft); Height: 4.65 m (15 ft); Wing area: 42.18 m² (454 sq ft)*

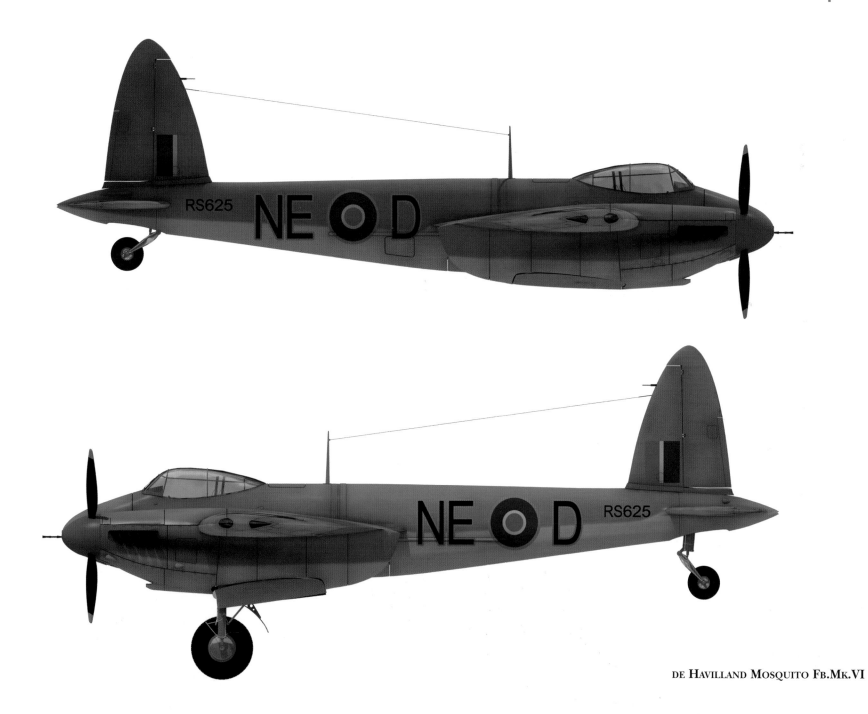

RS625

NE ● D

NE ● D

RS625

DE HAVILLAND MOSQUITO FB.MK.VI

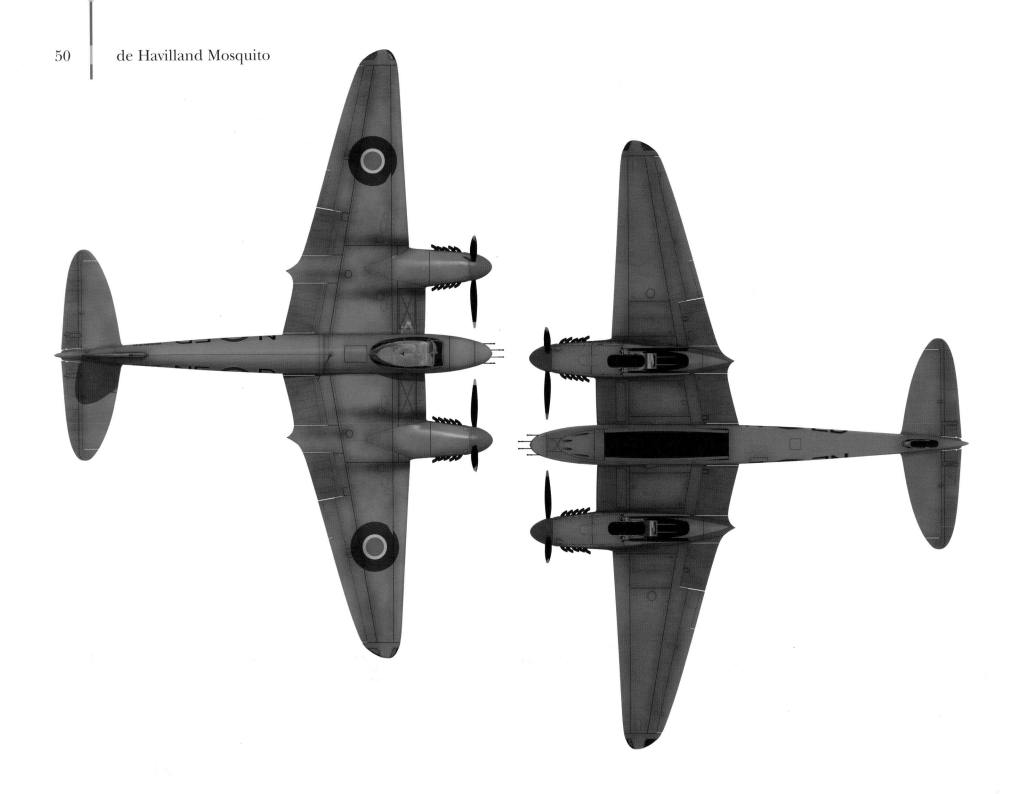

Targeting Enemy Shipping
*This Mosquito FB.Mk.VI served with No. 143
Squadron, an RAF Coastal Command unit that
formed part of the anti-shipping strike wing at Banff,
Scotland. Its main function was to attack enemy
shipping off the Norwegian coast.*

DISTINCTIVE FEATURES

The Mosquito's all-wood construction, as well as providing lightness and great strength, made the aircraft very hard to detect by radar. Coupled with its excellent performance at altitude, these attributes also made the Mosquito a useful reconnaissance aircraft. Illustrated here is a Mosquito PR.Mk.XVI – by far the most numerous photo reconnaissance version. To reduce the need for metal, and to minimize the machining required, the Mosquito's sturdy undercarriage featured rubber blocks in compression in place of oleo-pneumatic shock absorbers. Another of the Mosquito's recognition features was its distinctive wing planform, with engine nacelles extending forward of the fuselage nose.

Douglas A-20

The Douglas A-20 had its origins in the DB-7 attack bomber series, which began with the Model 7A, submitted in response to a 1938 US Army Air Corps requirement. The first prototype, designated Model 7B, flew on 26 October 1939; 100 examples were ordered by France in February 1940, and 186, designated A-20 and A-20A, by the USAAC three months later. These, with the manufacturer's designation DRB-7, had a narrower and deeper fuselage than the original model. France fell after 115 aircraft had been delivered, 95 of these surviving in North Africa; the rest were diverted to Britain, where they were converted into Havoc night fighters/intruders with 'solid' noses. The USAAC also converted 60 A-20s into P-70 'stopgap' night fighters. The RAF ultimately received 781 aircraft, named Boston III, while 808 similar aircraft were produced for the USAAC/USAAF as the A-20C. Of these, 202 went to the RAF as the Boston IIIA.

- The next major variant was the A-20G, 2850 being built with the 'solid' nose of the fighter variants and an increased bomb-carrying capacity. Later variants were the A-20J and A-20K, which had a moulded plastic one-piece transparent nose; these were designated Boston IV and V in RAF service.
- Total production of the DB-7 series, including the fighter variants, was 7385.
- Almost half of the DB-7 eries output went to the Soviet Union.

SPECIFICATIONS

TYPE: *Two-/three-seat light-attack bomber*

POWERPLANT: *Two 1193 kW (2,625 hp) Wright R-2800-23 Double Cyclone radial piston engines*

PERFORMANCE: *Maximum speed: 546 km/h (340 mph) at 3780 m (12,400 ft); Range: 1754 km (1,087 miles); Service ceiling: 7865 m (25,800 ft)*

WEIGHTS: *Empty: 7250 kg (14,950 lb); Loaded: 12,338 kg (27,144 lb)*

ARMAMENT: *Six forward-firing 12.7 mm (.50 cal.) machine guns in nose; two 12.7 mm machine guns in power-operated dorsal turret; one manual 12.7 mm machine gun in the ventral position; up to 1814 kg (3,990 lb) of bombs*

DIMENSIONS: *Span: 18.69 m (61 ft); Length: 14.63 m (48 ft); Height: 5.36 m (18 ft); Wing area: 43.11 m² (464 sq ft)*

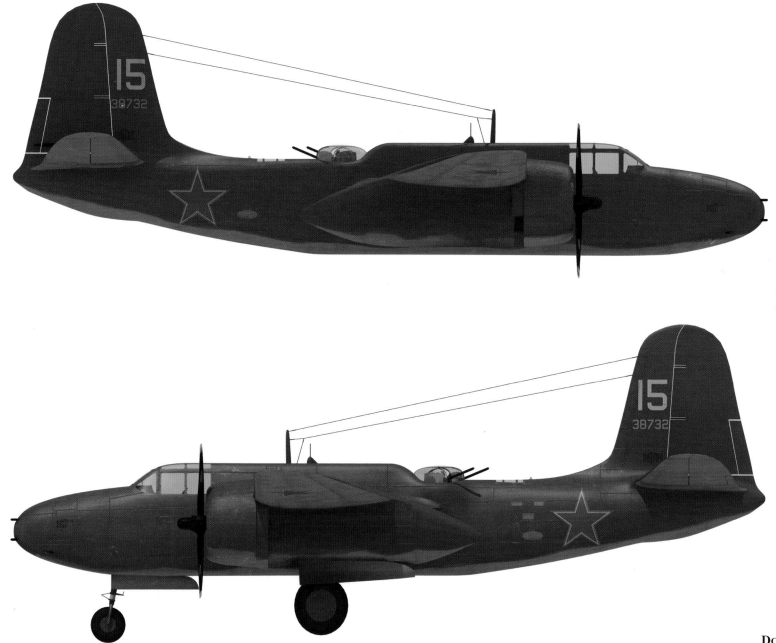

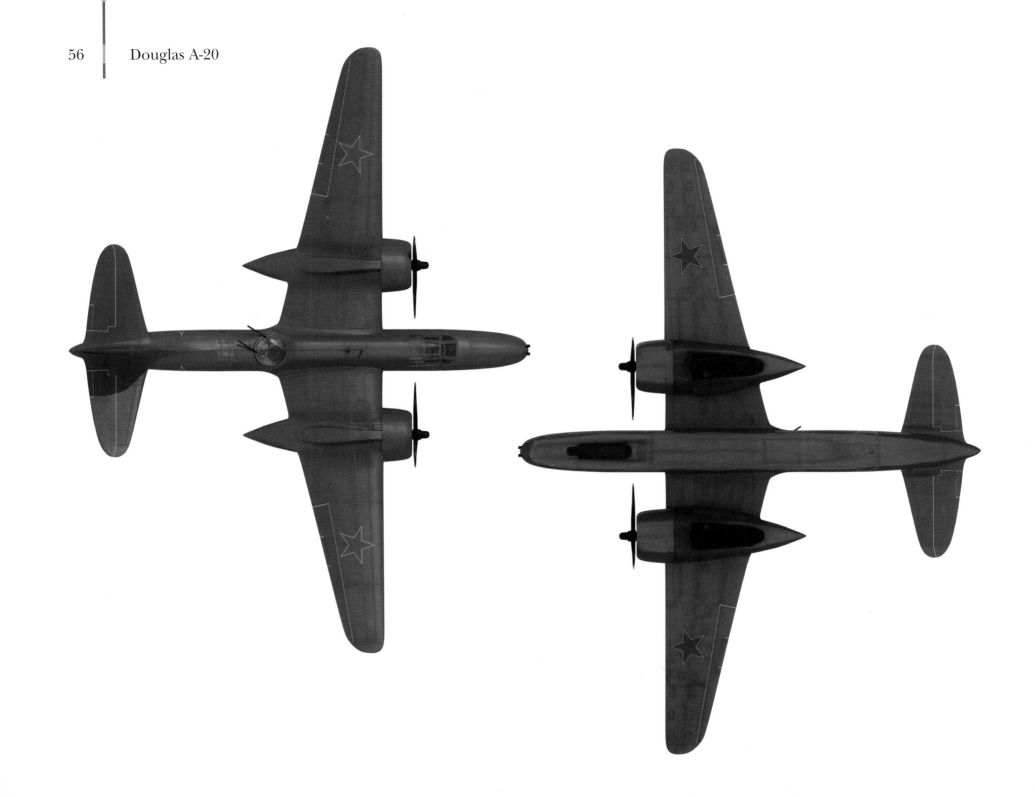

A Multitude of Roles

Some of the Soviet A-20s had their rear gun positions replaced by a Russian-built turret containing a single 12.7 mm (.50 cal.) Beresin BS machine gun. The Soviet A-20s were used in just about every conceivable role, ranging from tactical support of armoured units to torpedo bombers.

A RELIABLE PERFORMER

The A-20's armament varied, depending on operational requirements, with some having 7.63 mm (0.303 in) machine guns in blisters on the fuselage sides. Illustrated is an early DB-7 supplied to the RAF for training purposes only. The A-20's dorsal gunner sat in a relatively exposed position. The extreme conditions found in Russia meant that aircraft supplied to the Soviet Union were fitted with a fully enclosed ball-type dorsal turret. Although its wartime career was not particularly spectacular, the A-20 was popular with its pilots. The cockpit was roomy, with everything within easy reach, and the type was extremely rugged, versatile and dependable.

Fairey Swordfish

Affectionately know as the 'Stringbag', the Fairey Swordfish made a decisive contribution to the war, especially in the Mediterranean. The biplane torpedo-bomber served in all theatres. First flown on 17 April 1934, the Fairey TSR II, as the Swordfish was originally known, was a larger version of the private-venture TSR I. By the outbreak of World War II, 689 Swordfish had been delivered or were on order. The aircraft had a distinguished war career, its most notable action being the devastating torpedo attack on the Italian fleet at Taranto in November 1944. Other notable actions included the Battle of Cape Matapan in March 1941; the crippling of the German battleship *Bismarck* in May; and the gallant action against the *Scharnhorst*, *Gneisenau* and *Prinz Eugen* during the 'Channel Dash' of February 1942, when all six Swordfish of No. 825 Squadron involved were shot down, and Lt Cdr Eugene Esmonde was awarded a posthumous Victoria Cross.

- Thirteen Royal Navy squadrons were equipped with the type; a further 12 were formed during the war.
- The Swordfish Mk II, which appeared in 1943, had metal-covered lower wings, enabling it to carry rocket projectiles. Two German U-boats were sunk by Swordfish rocket attack, and the RPs were used against many other vessels in the closing months of the war.
- The Swordfish Mk III carried ASV radar in a housing between the main landing gear legs.

SPECIFICATIONS

TYPE: *Two-/three-seat torpedo-bomber/reconnaissance biplane*

POWERPLANT: *One 559 kW (750 hp) Bristol Pegasus XXX nine-cylinder radial piston engine*

PERFORMANCE: *Maximum speed: 222 km/h (138 mph); Range: 1658 km (1,028 miles); Service ceiling: 3260 m (10,690 ft)*

WEIGHTS: *Empty: 2132 kg (4,690 lb); Loaded: 3406 kg (7,493 lb)*

ARMAMENT: *One forward-firing 7.7 mm (.303 cal.) Vickers machine gun in fuselage and one 7.7 mm Lewis or Vickers 'K' gun mounted in rear cockpit; one 730 kg (1,600 lb) torpedo, or depth charges, mines or bombs up to 680 kg (1,500 lb), or eight rocket projectiles*

DIMENSIONS: *Span: 13.87 m (45 ft); Length: 10.87 m (36 ft); Height: 3.76 m (12 ft); Wing area: 56.39 m² (607 sq ft)*

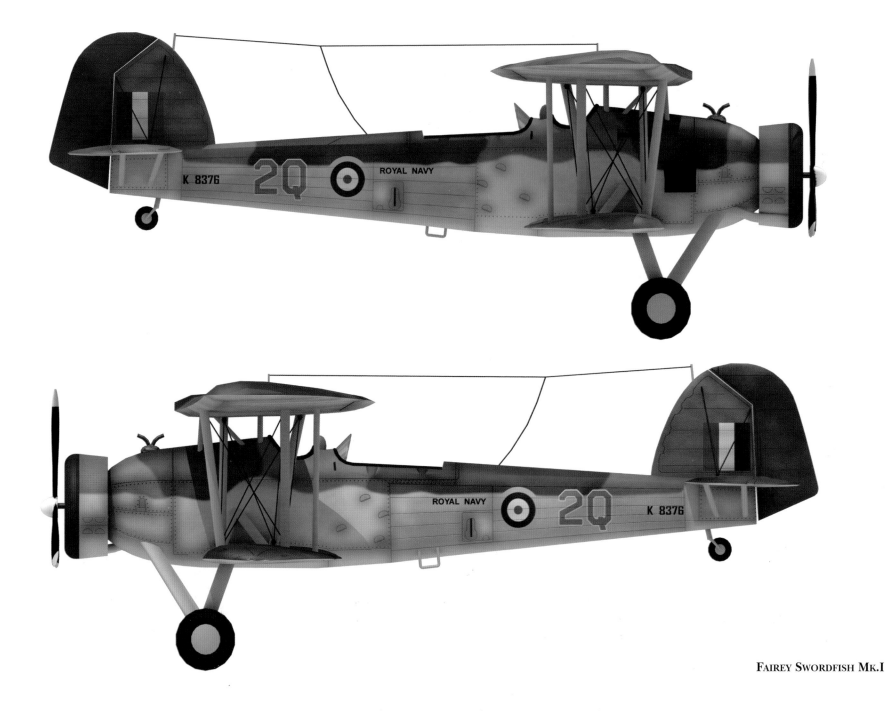

FAIREY SWORDFISH MK.I

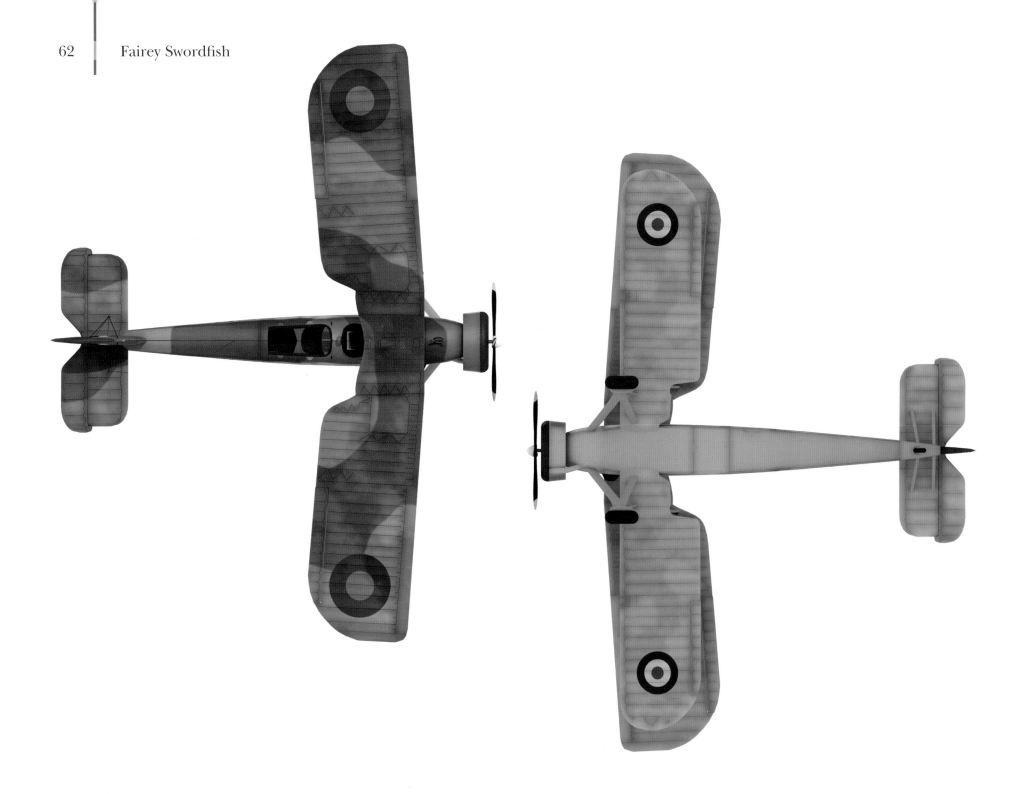

Torpedo Bombing
A Fairey Swordfish Mk.I carrying a 45.7 cm (18 in) torpedo. With a 226 kg (500 lb) warhead, the air-launched torpedo had become a formidable weapon by the time Germany and the Allies waged war in the Atlantic.

NIGHT DEVASTATION

Although criticized by many as outdated, the Fairey Swordfish proved its worth in the spectacular night attack on the Italian fleet at Taranto on 11 November 1940 by 21 Swordfish of Nos 815 and 819 squadrons from HMS Illustrious. Twelve of the Swordfish were armed with torpedoes; the others carried flares for target illumination, and bombs for use against oil installations on shore. The attack was brilliantly successful. At one stroke, the Italian battle fleet was reduced from six to three capital ships at a crucial period of the Mediterranean war, and for the loss of only two Swordfish. It was the first real demonstration of the aircraft carrier as a means of exercising flexible, mobile sea power, and the lesson was not lost on the Japanese Admiral Isoroku Yamamoto, whose carrier aircraft attacked Pearl Harbor a little more than a year later. This preserved Swordfish Mk.II is painted in the colours of 825 Naval Air Squadron, and played a starring role in the 1959 movie 'Sink The Bismarck!'

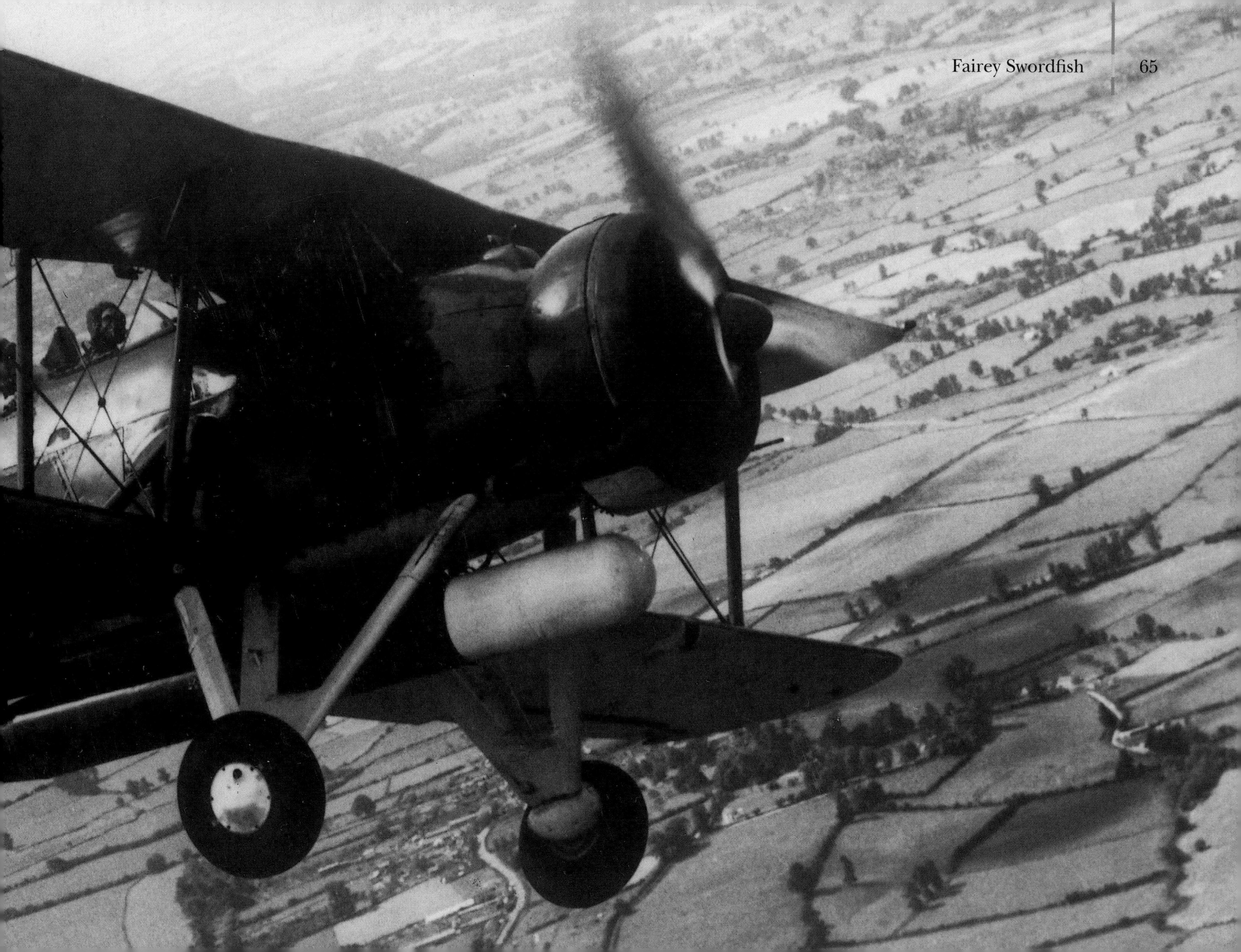

Focke-Wulf Fw 190

Known as the 'Butcher Bird' by many of its opponents, the Fw 190 made its appearance in the autumn of 1941 and for months established air superiority for the Luftwaffe. As the Fw 190 was encountered more frequently, it became apparent that it outclassed the Spitfire V in all aspects except radius of turn. The first major operation in which it was involved was the famous 'Channel Dash' on 12 February 1942, when the German battlecruisers *Scharnhorst* and *Gneisenau*, together with the heavy cruiser *Prinz Eugen*, made a fast passage from the French Atlantic port of Brest to northern Germany via the English Channel.

- The two Luftwaffe fighter wings based on the Channel coast of France, JG 2 and JG 26, rearmed with the Fw 190A-3 in June 1942 and began attacks on targets on the south coast of England.
- More than 20,000 Fw 190s were built in many subvariants, one being a fighter-bomber with provision for 1000 kg (2,205 lb) of bombs, and others being bomber-destroyers, with 30 mm (1.18 in) cannon and extra armour to protect the pilot in head-on attacks.
- The FW 190D, which entered service in 1943, had a lengthened nose accommodating a 1324 kW (1,776 hp) Junkers Jumo 213A-1 engine, a liquid-cooled unit fitted with an annular radiator duct.

SPECIFICATIONS

TYPE: *Single-seat fighter and fighter-bomber*

POWERPLANT: *One 1287 kW (1,725 hp) Junkers Jumo 213E inverted Vee piston engine*

PERFORMANCE: *Maximum speed: 685 km/h (426 mph); Service ceiling: 12,191 m (40,000 ft)*

WEIGHT: *Empty: 4839 kg (10,670 lb)*

ARMAMENT: *Two 13 mm (0.5 in) MG 131 machine guns; two 20 mm (0.79 in) MG 151/20 E cannon; one 500 kg (1,102 lb) bomb*

DIMENSIONS: *Span: 10.40 m (34 ft 5 in); Length: 10.10 m (33 ft 5 in); Height: 3.30 m (11 ft); Wing area: 18.30 m² (197 sq ft)*

Focke-Wulf Fw 190D-9

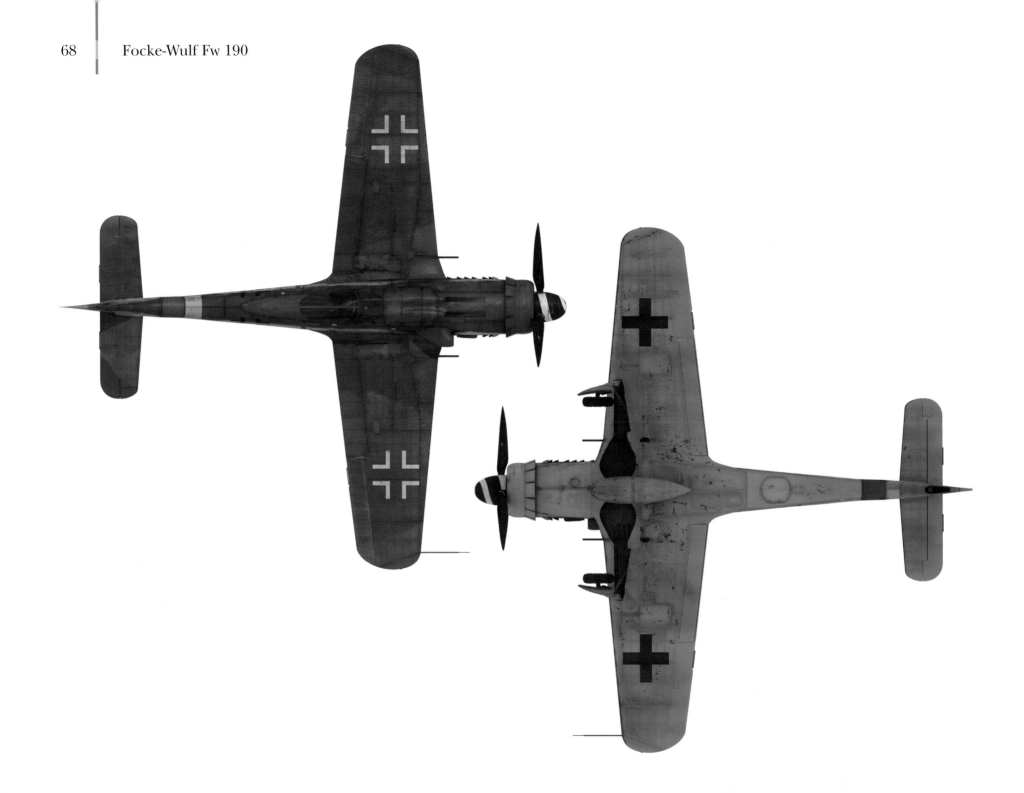

Night Fighting
This Fw 190D-9 'Dora' was operated by JG 301, a night fighter unit formed specifically for so-called 'Wilde Sau' (Wild Boar) operations. The idea was for the fighter pilots to attack RAF bombers silhouetted against the glare of burning cities.

LETHAL ADVERSARY

The wide-track undercarriage of the Focke-Wulf Fw 190 made it much more suitable than the Bf 109 for operations from rough and semi-prepared airstrips, and gave it more forgiving handling characteristics in the hands of inexperienced pilots. The Fw 190's one-piece, rearward-sliding canopy provided an excellent all-round view by the standards of the time. Combined with the aircraft's performance and agility, this feature made the 'Butcher Bird' a deadly adversary. The Fw 190 was so successful that the German Air Ministry allowed its designer, Kurt Tank, to use the first letters of his surname to prefix all subsequent Focke-Wulf designs. One was the Ta 152H, which was first issued to JG 301 early in 1945, its task being to protect the Me 262 jet fighter bases. About 150 examples were completed before the collapse of Germany brought an end to further production.

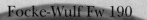

Grumman TBM-3 Avenger

The Grumman Avenger replaced the hopelessly outclassed Douglas Devastator as the US Navy's standard torpedo-bomber. Although it had a disastrous start to its operational career at the Battle of Midway in June 1942, when five out of six aircraft of Torpedo Squadron VT-8 were shot down in an attack on the Japanese task force, the Avenger went on to build a distinguished operational record and become one of the best shipborne torpedo-bombers of World War II. Many TBM-3 Avengers were supplied to the Royal Navy, which used them to attack enemy shipping in Arctic waters and the Far East, where Avenger squadrons were deployed with the British Task Force 57. Avengers also served with the French navy, which used them operationally during the Anglo-French invasion of the Suez Canal Zone in November 1956.

- The Avenger was a very robust aircraft. Its fuselage was of oval section and semi-monocoque construction, built up from a series of angle frames and stamped bulkheads, all covered by a smooth metal skin.
- The TBM-3F version had an uprated Wright Cyclone engine and strengthened wings to support rocket projectiles or a radar pod.
- The TBF usually carried a crew of three. The pilot fired the fixed forward-firing guns and released the torpedo. The bomb aimer's position was in the lower fuselage, aft of the bomb bay; he also operated the ventral gun. The radio operator, who was aft of the pilot, also served as the turret gunner.

SPECIFICATIONS

TYPE: *Three-seat carrier-based torpedo-bomber*

POWERPLANT: *One 1268 kW (1,700 hp) Wright R-2600-20 Cyclone 14-cylinder radial piston engine*

PERFORMANCE: *Maximum speed: 436 km/h (270 mph) at 5030 m (15,000 ft); Range: 1778 km (1,100 miles); Service ceiling: 6830 m (22,400 ft)*

WEIGHTS: *Empty: 4788 kg (10,534 lb); Maximum take-off: 7876 kg (17,327 lb)*

ARMAMENT: *Two fixed forward-firing 12.7 mm (.50 cal.) machine guns; one 12.7 mm machine gun in rear turret, one 7.62 mm (.30 cal.) machine gun in ventral position; 907 kg (2,000 lb) of bombs or one torpedo in internal bomb-bay*

DIMENSIONS: *Span: 16.51 m (54 ft 2 in); Length: 12.20 m (40 ft); Height: 5.00 m (16 ft 5 in); Wing area: 45.52 m² (490 sq ft)*

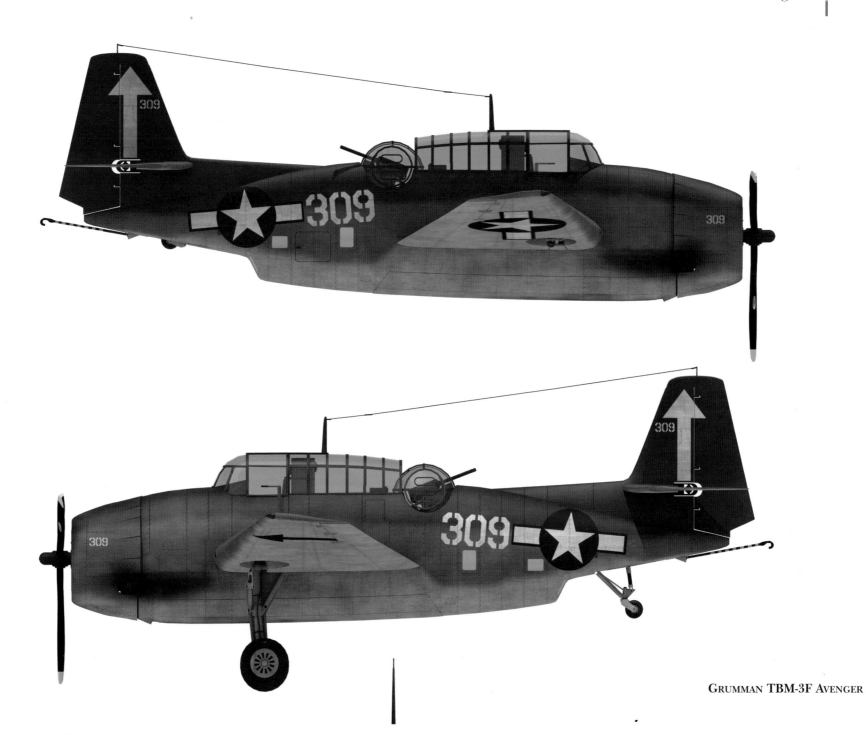

GRUMMAN TBM-3F AVENGER

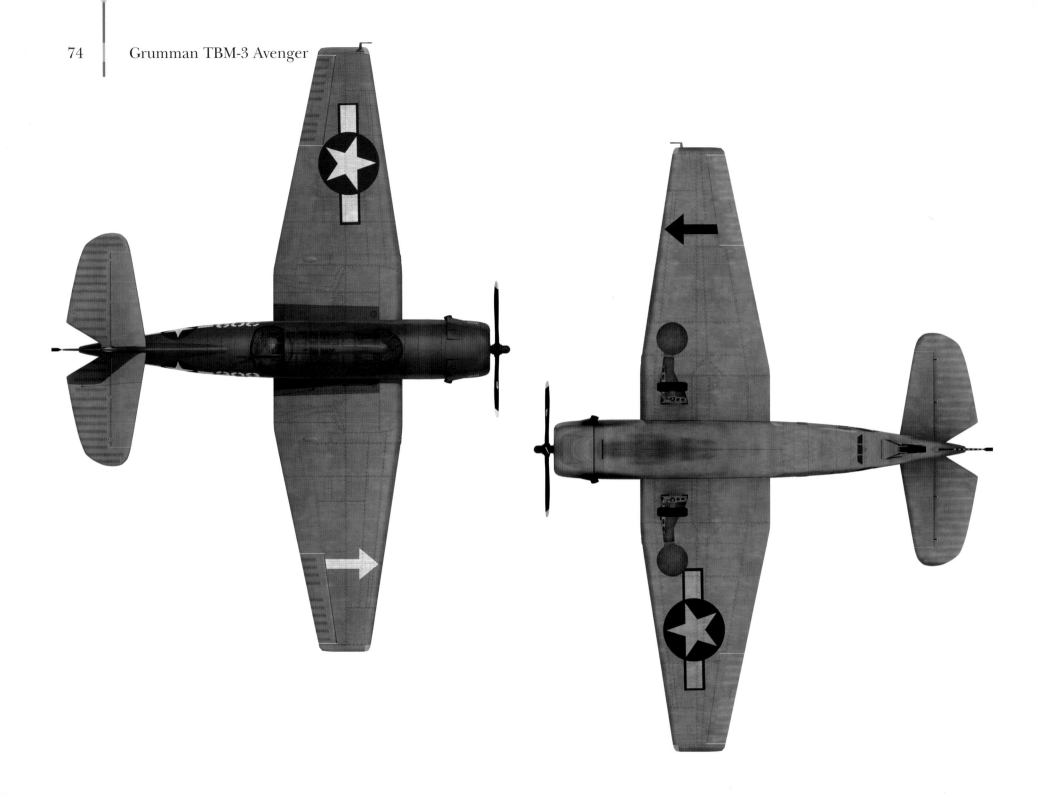

Destroying the Japanese Navy

A Grumman TBM-3F Avenger of US Navy Torpedo Squadron VT-83, which served on the USS Essex in the Pacific war. After an inauspicious combat debut, the Avenger went on to play a leading part in the destruction of the Imperial Japanese Navy.

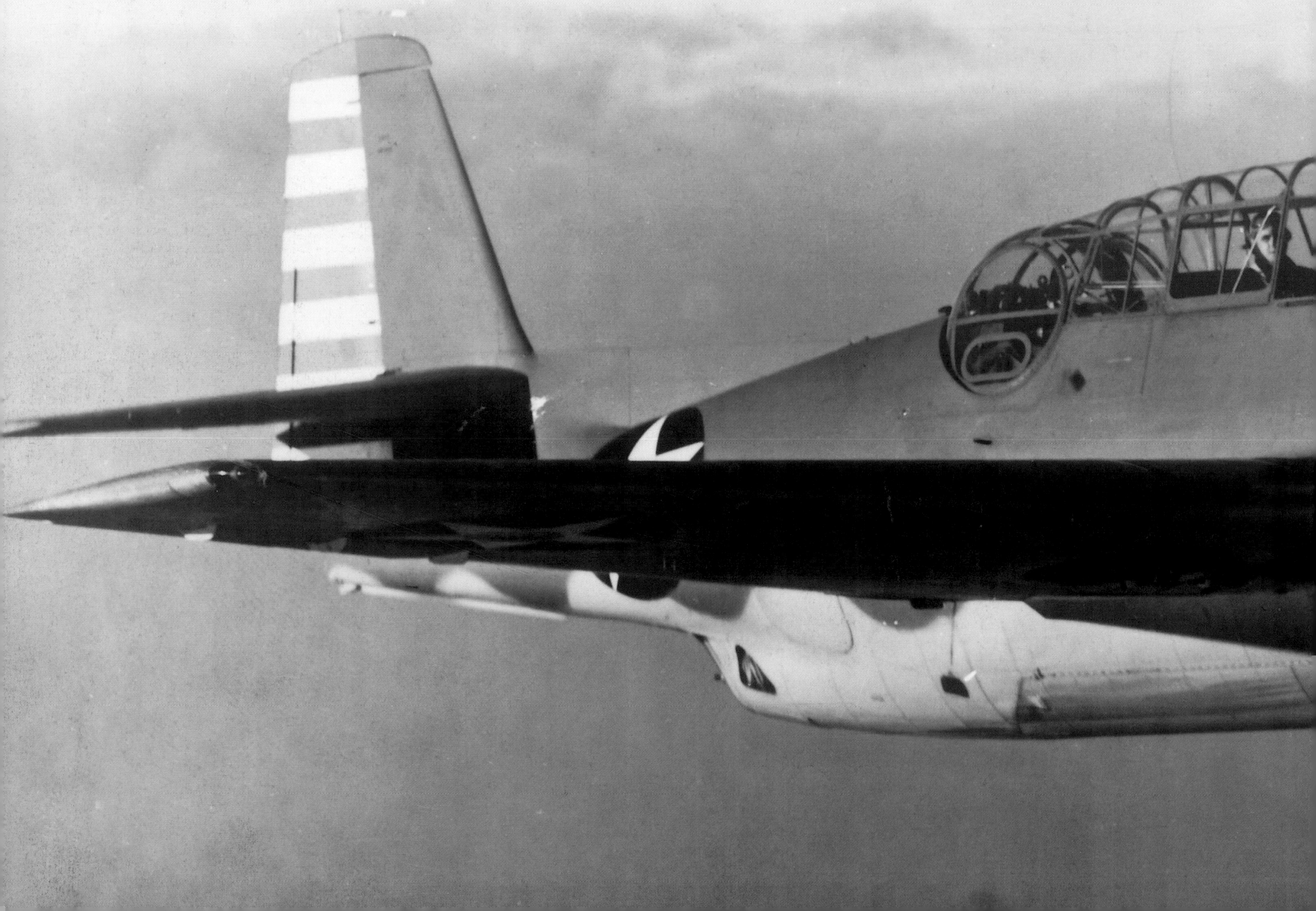

GROWING SUCCESS

The losses suffered by the US Navy's Avengers cast serious doubts on the viability of the torpedo attack concept, but faith in it was soon restored by the Avenger's successes in later battles, especially as more reliable torpedoes became available. Avengers took part in almost every Pacific war battle from Midway to the end, operating from land bases on Guadalcanal and other islands, as well as from aircraft carriers. They operated mainly as bombers rather than torpedo strike aircraft, and proved invaluable in other roles such as search and rescue. On 7 April 1945, Avengers attacked and sank the world's largest battleship, the Yamato, *which had sailed on a suicide mission to attack US forces off Okinawa, hitting her with 10 torpedoes.*

Grumman F6F Hellcat

The Grumman Hellcat has an assured place in history as the fighter that changed the course of the Pacific air war. The appearance of the Hellcat in 1943 changed the picture completely, the robust US fighter establishing a kill ratio in the region of 19:1. It went on to play a prominent role in all US naval operations. Its greatest success came during the Battle of the Philippine Sea in June 1944, when carrier-based aircraft provided air cover for the occupation of the Marianas. The great air battle that followed was a one-sided massacre that would go down in history as the 'Marianas Turkey Shoot'. US combat air patrols and anti-aircraft fire destroyed 325 enemy aircraft, including 220 of the 328 launched by Japanese aircraft carriers. US losses were 16 Hellcats in combat; seven other aircraft shot down by Japanese fighters or ground fire.

- Before the Hellcat made its operational debut over Marcus Island on 31 August 1943, operating with Navy Fighter Squadron VF-5 from the USS *Yorktown*, it was the Mitsubishi Zero that ruled the Pacific sky.
- The Hellcat flew for the first time on 26 June 1942, its design having benefited from combat lessons learned by its predecessor, the Wildcat.
- First deliveries of the F6F-3 Hellcat were made to US Navy Fighter Squadron VF-9 aboard the aircraft carrier USS *Essex* on 16 January 1943.

SPECIFICATIONS

Type: *Single-seat carrier-based fighter*

Powerplant: *One 1492 kW (2,000 hp) Pratt & Whitney R-2800-10W Double Wasp 18-cylinder radial piston engine*

Performance: *Maximum speed: 620 km/h (380 mph) at medium altitude; Range: 1675 km (1,040 miles); Service ceiling: 11,500 m (37,500 ft)*

Weights: *Empty: 4191 kg (9,200 lb); Loaded: 6991 kg (15,400 lb)*

Armament: *Six 12.7 mm (.50 cal.) Browning M2 machine guns; up to 907 kg (2,000 lb) of bombs; six 127 mm (5 in) rockets*

Dimensions: *Span: 13.08 m (42 ft 10 in); Length: 10.23 m (33 ft 7 in); Height: 3.99 m (13 ft 1 in); Wing area: 31.03 m² (334 sq ft)*

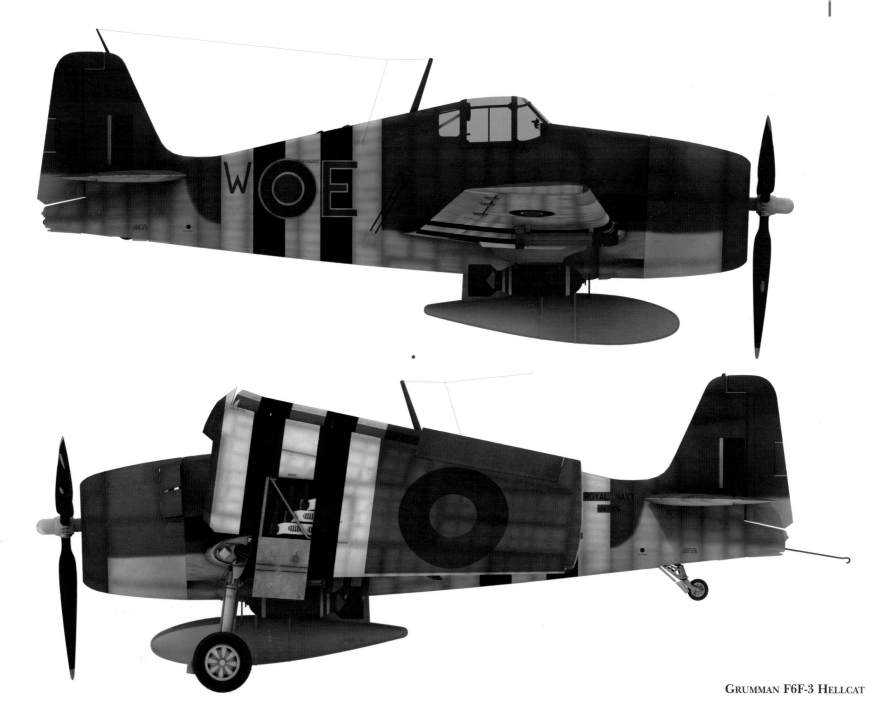

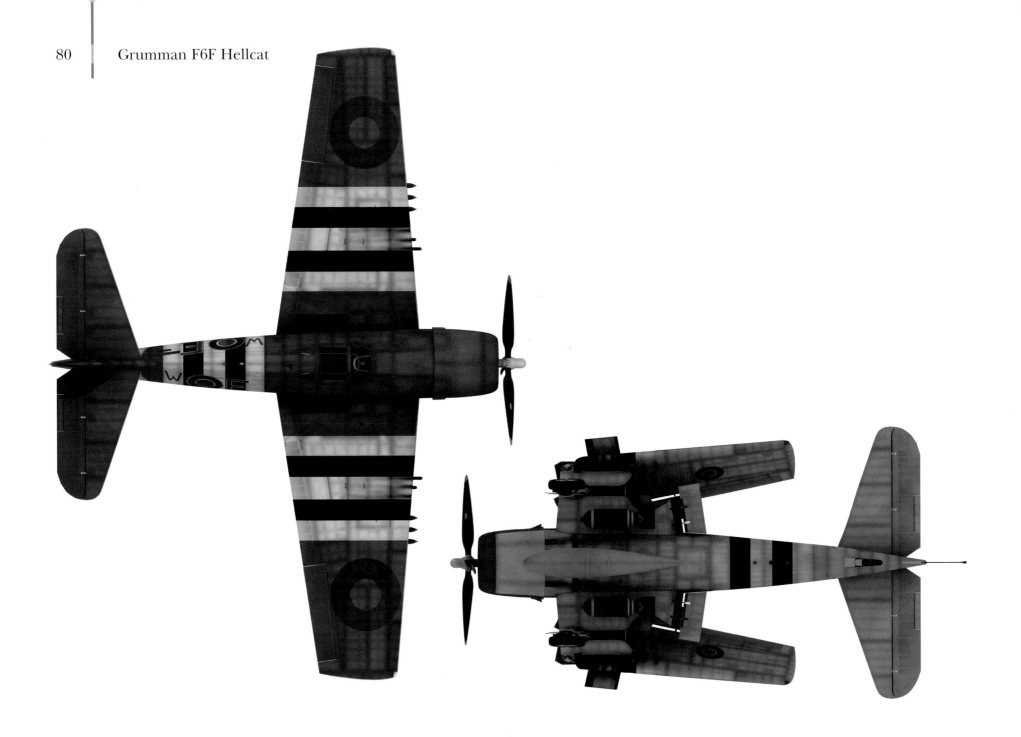

Serving with the Royal Navy
The Royal Navy was a major user of the Grumman Hellcat. This example carries the D-Day markings of No. 800 Squadron, Fleet Air Arm, the first Royal Navy squadron to receive the American type.

TURNING THE TIDE

Almost all Grumann Hellcats were armed with six Browning 12.7 mm (0.50 in) machine guns mounted in the wings, slightly staggered and armed with 400 rounds per gun. The 127 mm (5 in) rocket was a favoured weapon for ground attack in the later stages of World War II. Thousands were expended in the attacks on Iwo Jima and Okinawa. Six could be carried by the Hellcat. The pilot sat under a sliding canopy and was well protected by armour, particularly to the rear. No rearview mirror was provided, however, and rearward visibility was lacking. The Hellcat squadrons in the Pacific destroyed more enemy aircraft than any other Allied type, although by the time they became operational the best of the Imperial Japanese Navy's aircrews had already been killed.

Hawker Hurricane

Although overshadowed in the Battle of Britain by the more glamorous Spitfire, the Hawker Hurricane continued to prove its worth as a fighter-bomber in other theatres of war. Production Hurricane Is were delivered to No. 111 Squadron RAF at Northolt in November 1935. In 1938 the first deliveries were made to foreign customers (Portugal, Yugoslavia, Persia and Belgium). Hurricanes were also exported to Romania and Turkey. The type would almost certainly have been the subject of huge export orders had it not been for the outbreak of war in 1939. RAF Hurricanes fought in Norway, France, the Battle of Britain, North Africa (where it was used effectively as a tank-buster, armed with 40 mm/1.57 in cannon), Greece and Burma.

- One major user of the Hurricane was the Soviet Union. The first batch to be delivered comprised 24 Mk IIBs turned over to the Soviet navy's 72nd Fighter Air Regiment by No. 141 Wing RAF, which operated in North Russia in the late summer of 1941. Altogether, the Soviets received 2952 Hurricanes.
- In 1941 the Hurricane was adopted by the Royal Navy for fleet protection duties, with the first Sea Hurricanes being deployed on escort carriers.
- The Hurricane really came into its own during the Burma Campaign, as a tactical support aircraft armed with a pair of 227 kg (500 lb) bombs.

SPECIFICATIONS

TYPE: *Single-seat fighter-bomber*

POWERPLANT: *One 954 kW (1,280 hp) Rolls-Royce Merlin XX liquid-cooled piston engine*

PERFORMANCE: *Maximum speed: 541 km/h (335 mph); Range: 740 km (460 miles) or 1480 km (920 miles) with two 200 litre (53 gallon) drop tanks; Service ceiling: 10,850 m (35,600 ft)*

WEIGHTS: *Empty: 2631 kg (5,788 lb); Loaded: 3674 kg (8,083 lb)*

ARMAMENT: *Four Hispano or Oerlikon 20 mm (0.79 in) cannon and underwing racks for two 113 kg (250 lb) or 227 kg (500 lb) bombs*

DIMENSIONS: *Span: 12.19 m (40 ft); Length: 9.75 m (32 ft); Height: 3.99 m (13 ft 1 in); Wing area: 23.92 m² (257 sq ft)*

HAWKER HURRICANE MK I

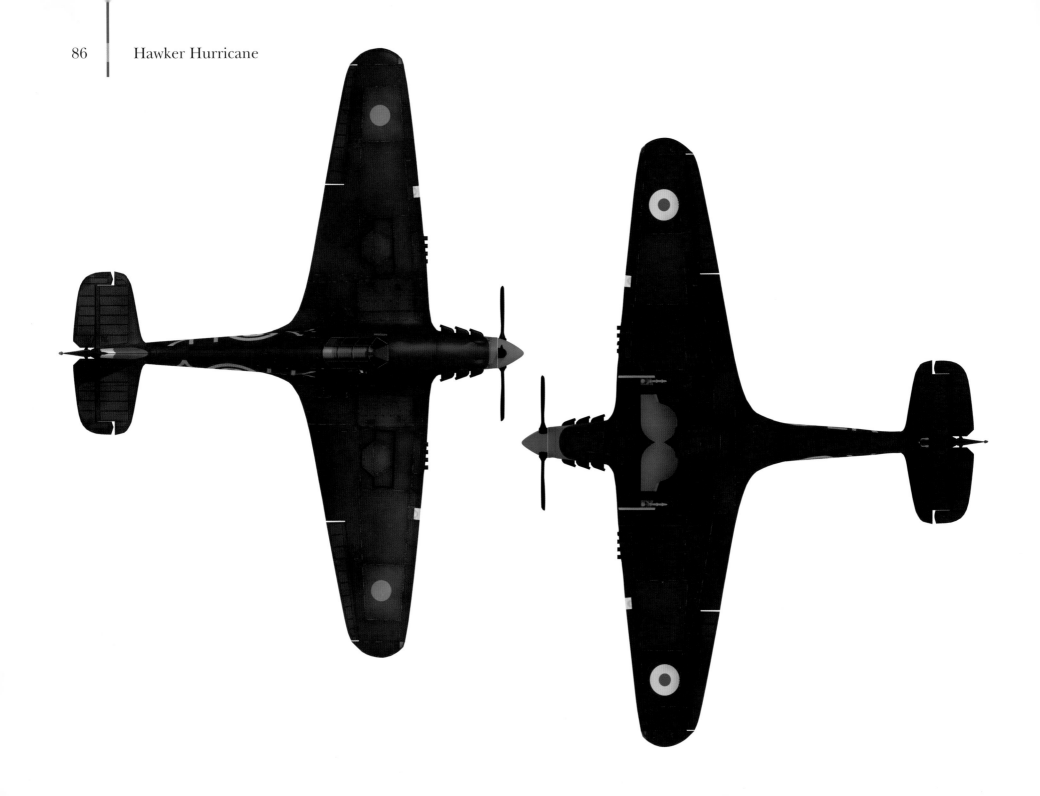

Commanding Officer's Mount
Hawker Hurricane Mk I flown by Sqn Ldr Ian 'Widge' Gleed, Officer Commanding No. 87 Squadron RAF, Charmy Down, Somerset, in December 1940. The blue and red bands on the rudder denote that this is the CO's personal aircraft.

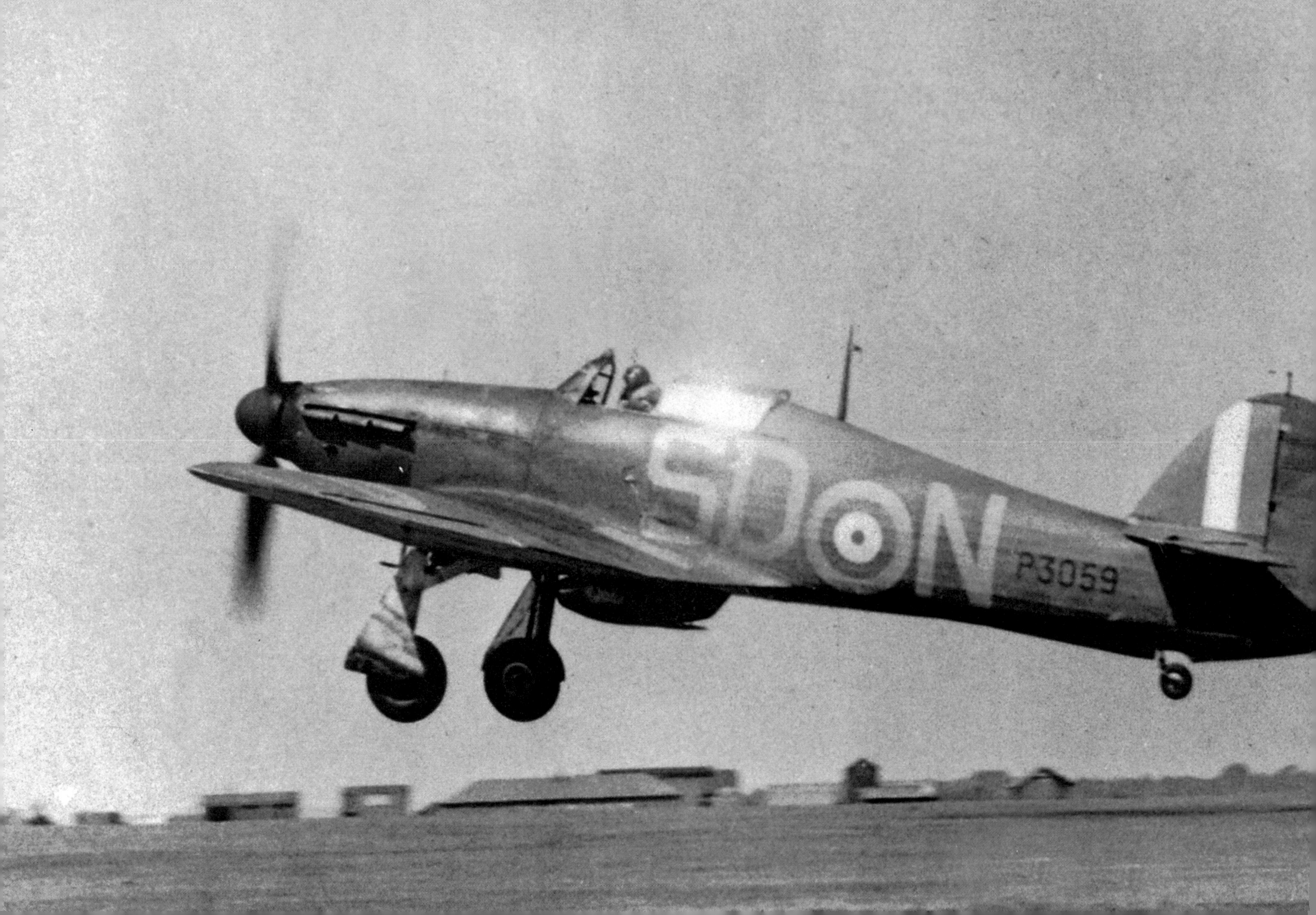
SD N
P3059

RUGGED AND RELIABLE

The Hawker Hurricane's fuselage was a box structure of round-section steel and duralumin type, wire-braced, and connected by wooden stringers attached to 11 tapering metal frames. The structure was covered with doped Irish linen. It was capable of absorbing an enormous amount of damage, and the airframe was easily repairable, unlike that of the all-metal Spitfire. The Hurricane also had a wide-track undercarriage, enabling it to operate from rough airstrips and from the decks of aircraft carriers without experiencing undue problems. This was one aspect of the Hurricane which the Russian pilots who flew it liked, although they did find the British fighter heavy to handle after lighter Russian fighters such as the Yak-1.

Hawker Typhoon

Intended as an all-altitude interceptor, the Hawker Typhoon proved inadequate in this role except at low level, but it went on to make its mark in history as the most potent Allied fighter-bomber. Two separate designs were submitted, the Type R and Type N. The Type N, named Typhoon, was selected. It was powered by a 1566 kW (2,100 hp) Napier Sabre H-type in-line engine, and the first of two prototypes flew for the first time on 24 February 1940. The type suffered from constant teething troubles, however, and the first RAF Typhoon squadron (No. 56) did not become operational until May 1942, being assigned to air defence operations against low-level intruders. The Typhoon MK 1A, armed with twelve 7.7 mm (0.303 in) machine guns, soon gave way to the Mk 1B, whose four 20 mm (0.79 in) cannon proved highly effective in the ground-attack role and which was powered by a more reliable 1626 kW (2,180 hp) Sabre IIA engine.

- The Typhoon was a cantilever low-wing monoplane of basically all-metal stressed-skin construction with a retractable tailwheel.
- It was designed to combat heavily armed and armoured escort fighters such as the Messerschmitt Bf 110.
- Later Typhoons had a clear bubble-type sliding canopy, in place of the original metal-framed cockpit.

SPECIFICATIONS

TYPE: *Single-seat fighter-bomber*

POWERPLANT: *One 1626 kW (2,180 hp) Napier Sabre IIA inline piston engine*

PERFORMANCE: *Maximum speed: 664 km/h (413 mph) at 6000 m (19,685 ft); Range: 975 km (606 miles) or 1500 km (932 miles) with drop-tanks; Service ceiling: 10,700 m (35,100 ft)*

WEIGHTS: *Empty: 3992 kg (8,800 lb); Loaded: 6010 kg (13,250 lb)*

ARMAMENT: *Four 20 mm (0.79 in) Hispano cannon each with 140 rounds; two bombs of up to 454 kg (1,000 lb) each; numerous other combinations including eight or 12 27 kg (60 lb) rockets or two 205 litre (45 gallon) drop-tanks*

DIMENSIONS: *Span: 12.67 m (41 ft 7 in); Length: 9.73 m (31 ft 11 in); Height: 4.52 m (14 ft 10 in); Wing area: 25.90 m² (279 sq ft)*

Hawker Typhoon Mk 1B

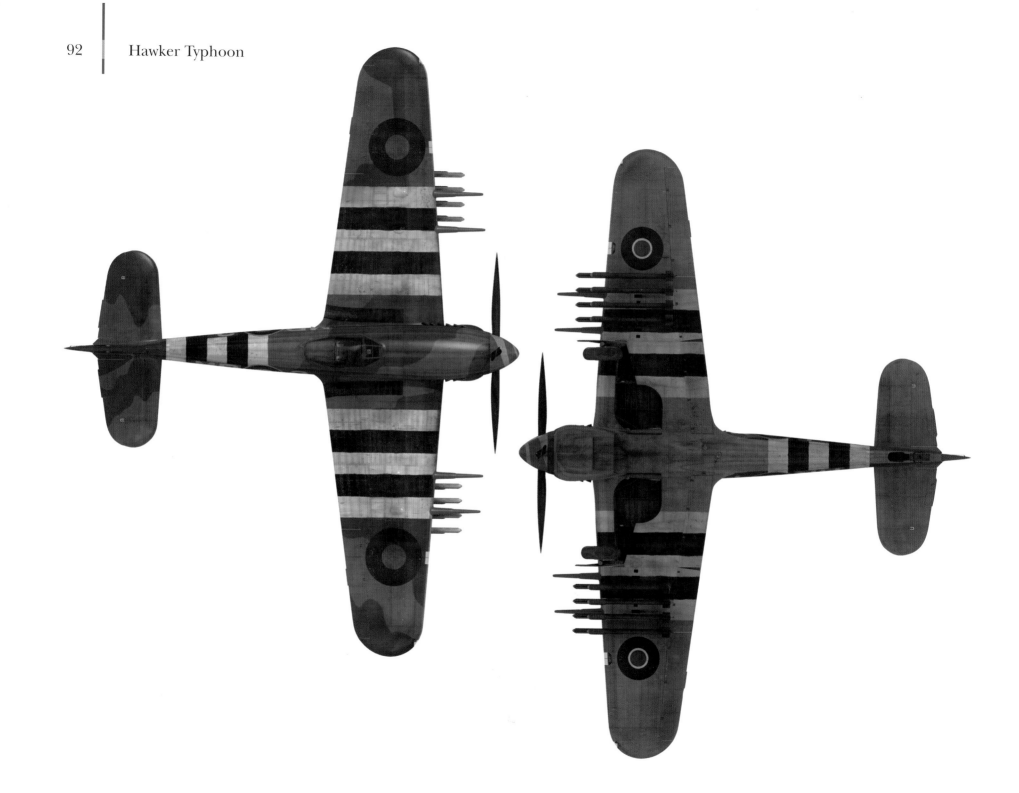

Supporting Ground Forces
A Hawker Typhoon Mk 1B of No. 245 Squadron RAF, 2nd Tactical Air Force, which flew ground-attack missions in support of the British Second Army in northwest Europe from D-Day in 1944 until the end of the war in Europe.

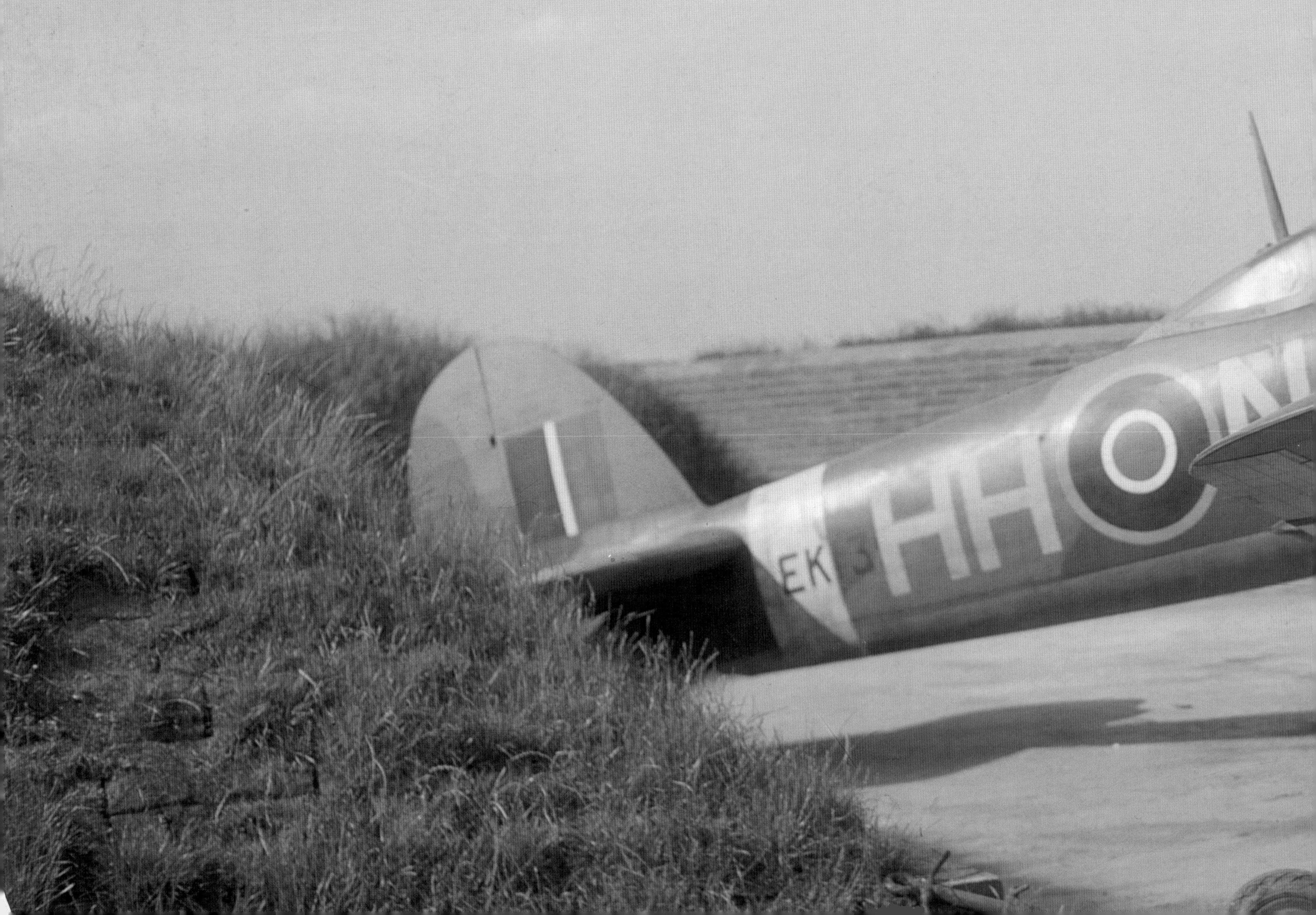
EK
HH

A POWERFUL TOOL

A rare wartime colour photograph of a Hawker Typhoon Mk 1B serves to illustrate the large size of the aircraft. By the end of 1943, with the aircraft's technical problems cured and the growing number of Typhoon squadrons – now carrying a pair of 226 kg (500 lb) bombs or eight underwing rocket projectiles on their aircraft in addition to the built-in cannon armament – striking hard at the enemy's communications, shipping and airfields, the aircraft really began to make its mark. After the Allied landings in Normandy, the name of the rocket-armed Typhoon became synonymous with the breakup of an enemy armoured counterattack at Mortain and the destruction of the retreating German army at Falaise. In the last days of World War II, having supported the Canadian 1st and British 2nd armies in their drive through northwest Europe, its final actions were against enemy shipping in the Baltic.

Heinkel He 111

The Heinkel He 111 was the backbone of the Luftwaffe's bomber force from 1939–43. During early operations against Poland, He 111 losses were comparatively light, but it was a different story when they encountered determined opposition during the Battle of France, and even more so in the Battle of Britain. One major mission undertaken by the He 111 was on the night of 21/22 June 1944. He 11s of KGs 4, 27, 53 and 55 attacked the Russian airfield of Poltava, where 114 USAAF B-17s and their P-51 fighter escort had landed after an attack on Berlin earlier in the day. The German bombers destroyed 43 Fortresses and 15 Mustangs.

- In 1937 an early version, the He 111B-1, was tested under combat conditions with the Condor Legion in Spain and proved very successful, its speed alone enabling it to evade fighter interception.
- The He 111 scored some notable successes against the Arctic convoys to Russia, notably against the ill-fated PQ17 in July 1942, when the convoy was virtually destroyed.
- He 111s were also used to launch V-1 flying bombs from over the North Sea at targets in the United Kingdom towards the end of 1944. These operations cost the launcher units 77 aircraft from July 1944 to January 1945, many the victims of Mosquito night fighters.

SPECIFICATIONS

Type: *Four-/five-seat medium bomber*

Powerplant: *Two 1006 kW (1,350 hp) Junkers Jumo 211F-2 inline piston engines*

Performance: *Maximum speed: 435 km/h (270 mph) at 6000 m (20,000 ft) (light load); Range: 1950 km (1,200 miles); Service ceiling: 8500 m (28,000 ft)*

Weights: *Empty: 8680 kg (19,096 lb); Loaded: 14,000 kg (30,800 lb)*

Armament: *One 20 mm (0.79 in) cannon, one 13 mm (0.51 in) and up to nine 7.92 mm (0.31 in) machine guns, plus provision for up to 3307 kg (7,275 lb) of bombs carried internally and externally*

Dimensions: *Span: 22.60 m (74 ft 1 in); Length: 16.40 m (53 ft 9 in); Height: 4.00 m (13 ft 1 in); Wing area: 86.50 m² (931 sq ft)*

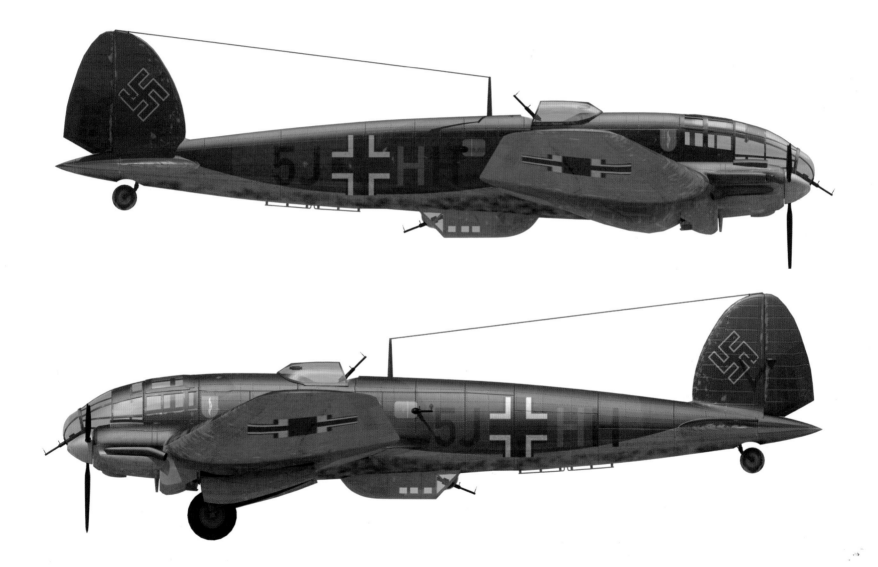

HEINKEL HE 111H

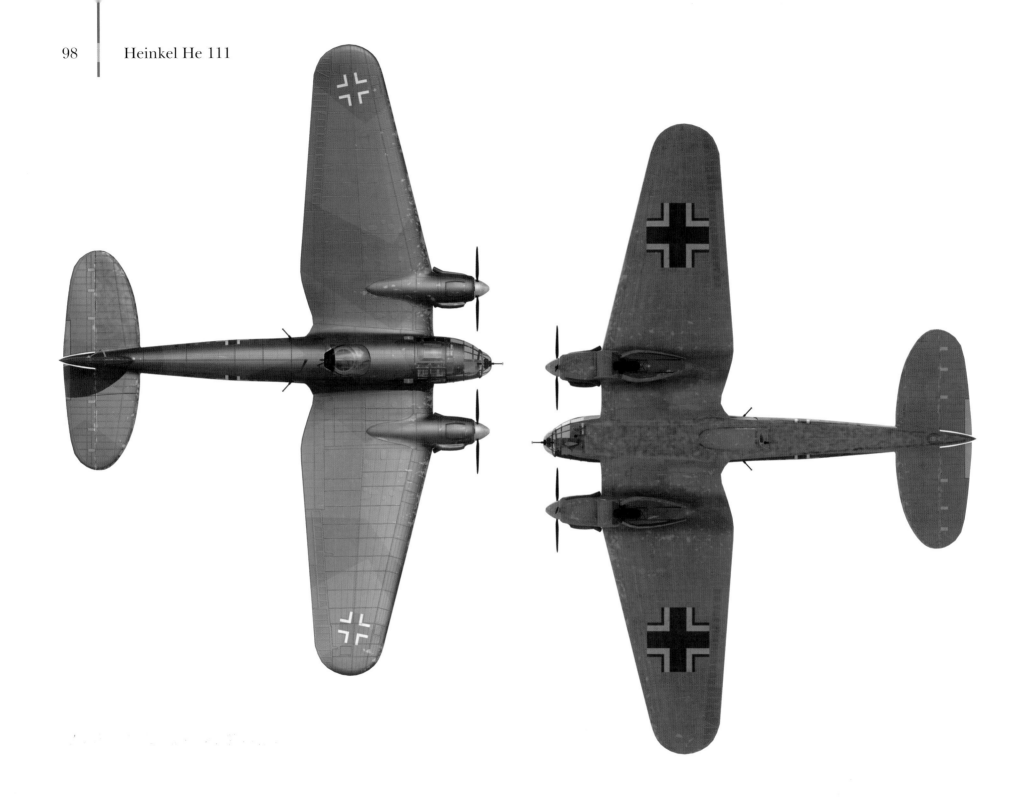

War-long Endurance
A Heinkel He 111H of Kampfgeschwader (KG) 4. This unit took part in the Luftwaffe's offensive in western Europe in 1940, and was the only He 111 bomber unit still operational at the end of the war in May 1945.

LACK OF ARMAMENT

As the He 111 was gradually withdrawn from frontline bomber operations, it was assigned to transport duties, and was heavily involved in attempting to fly supplies to the besieged German Sixth Army at Stalingrad during the winter of 1942–3. It was also used to drop paratroops behind enemy lines during the battle of the Ardennes in December 1944. One of the He 111's main problems that it was underarmed, and efforts to increase its defensive weaponry and armour plating resulted in an aircraft that became unacceptably heavy as the war progressed.

Ilyushin Il-2 Shturmovik

Destined to become one of the most famous ground-attack aircraft of all time, the Ilyushin Il-2 completed its State Acceptance Trials in March 1941 and was ordered into full production; 249 were produced before the German invasion of June 1941. It suffered serious losses in its early operational career, mainly because it lacked a rear gun position. A much-modified single-seater with heavier armament, the Il-2M, began to reach frontline units in the autumn of 1942, but it was not until August 1943 that a two-seater version appeared. This was the Il-2m3, which played a prominent, often decisive part in campaigns on the Eastern Front. By the winter of 1943–44, vast numbers of Il-2m3s were in service, equipping units of the Soviet naval air arm, as well as the Soviet air force. Naval Il-2s were used extensively for attacks on shipping in the Baltic and Black Sea. An improved version of the Il-2, the Il-10, entered service in the autumn of 1944.

- A staggering total of 36,183 Il-2s were built, more than any other type of aircraft in history.
- Both the Il-2 and Il-10 saw action over Germany during the closing weeks of World War II.
- In the post-war years, the Il-10 saw widespread service with Soviet Bloc air forces, some seeing action during the Korean War.

SPECIFICATIONS

TYPE: *One-/two-seat armoured close-support aircraft*

POWERPLANT: *One 1282 kW (1,720 hp) Mikulin AM-38F piston engine*

PERFORMANCE: *Maximum speed: 430 km/h (267 mph) at 6700 m (22,000 ft); Range: 600 km (375 miles); Service ceiling: 9700 m (31,825 ft) or 6500 m (21,320 ft) with bombload*

WEIGHTS: *Empty: 3250 kg (7,150 lb); Loaded: 5872 kg (12,920 lb)*

ARMAMENT: *Two 20 mm (0.79 in) and/or two 37 mm (1.47 in) cannon in wings and one manually aimed 12.7 mm (.50 cal.) machine gun in rear cockpit, plus 600 kg (1,320 lb) of bombs, or eight RS-82 or four RS-132 rockets under outer wing*

DIMENSIONS: *Span: 14.60 m (48 ft); Length: 11.65 m (38 ft); Height: 3.40 m (11 ft); Wing area: 38.50 m² (414 sq ft)*

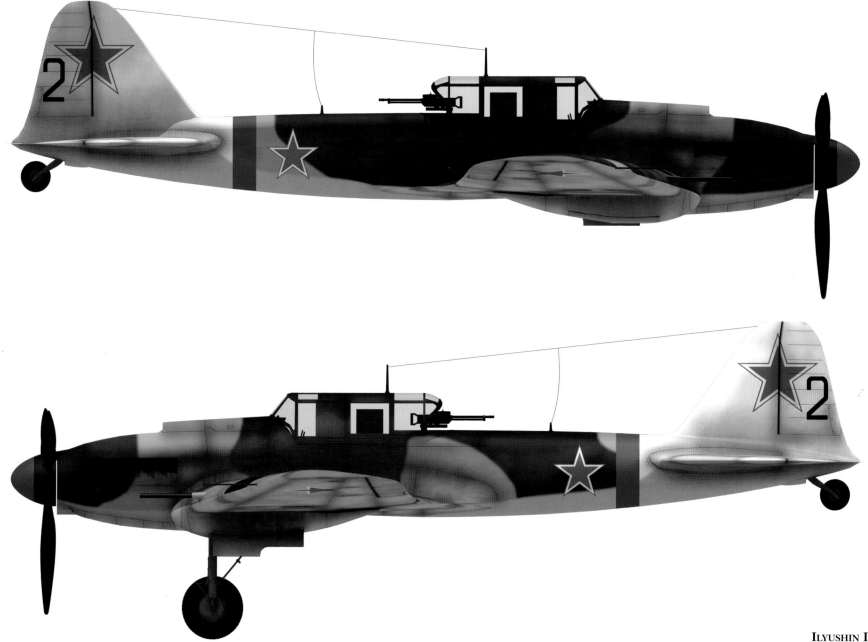

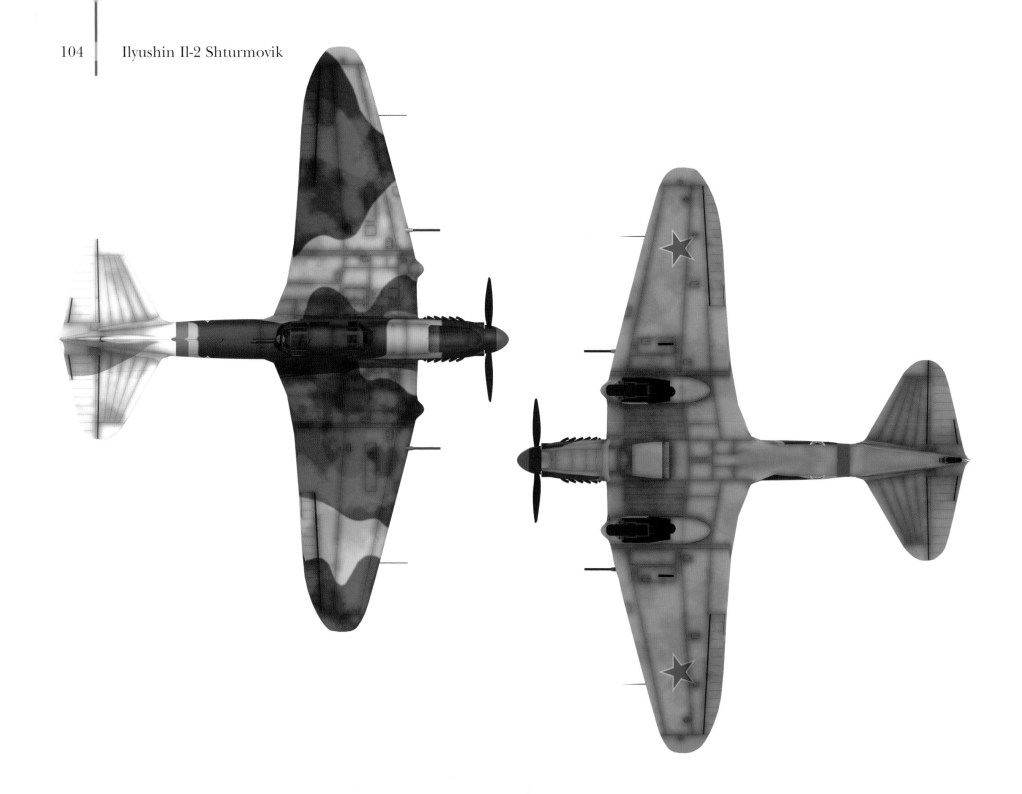

Il-2 Flying Ace
This Il-2 of the 2nd Squadron, 198th Assault Aviation Regiment, 233rd Air Division, was flown by Captain A.N. Yefimov, one of the Soviet air force's leading ground-attack exponents. He was twice awarded the gold star of a Hero of the Soviet Union.

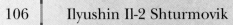

DEADLY TANK BUSTER

The Il-2M version of the famous Sturmovik appeared in 1942, its defensive capability increased by the addition of a rear gun position. The Il-2's armament was progressively improved as the war went on, 32mm (1.26 in) and 37mm (1.46 in) cannon being added to provide greater hitting power against a new generation of German tanks. The P-37 Nudelman-Suranov automatic cannon proved very effective against German armour at Kursk in the summer of 1943.

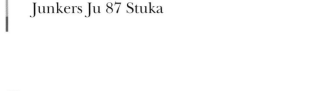

Junkers Ju 87 Stuka

The word 'Stuka' was applied to all German bomber aircraft with a dive-bombing capability during World War II, but it will always be associated with the Junkers Ju 87. In 1943 the Ju 87G 'tank buster' version appeared, armed with two 37 mm (1.46 in) cannon in pods under the wings. Its role was amply vindicated during the Battle of Kursk in July that year. Production of the Ju 87G was increased in the summer of 1944. The increasingly dire situation on the Russian front meant that the Germans needed as many anti-tank aircraft as they could muster to counter the Soviet armoured offensives. As the Russians now had air superiority, anti-tank aircraft had to be heavily escorted by fighters to have any hope of surviving.

- On 5 July 1943, Stuka ace Hans-Ulrich Rudel, flying a pre-production Ju 87G-0, attacked a column of 12 Russian T-34 tanks. Aiming for the lightly armoured rear area, he single-handedly destroyed them all.
- Rudel's and other successes against Russian armour led to the construction of the improved Ju 87G-1 and G-2 production models, and to Rudel being asked to form a special anti-tank unit.
- This anti-tank unit, designated 10 (Pz)/St.G2, was equipped with the Ju 87G-1; further successes led to a second unit, III/St.G2, being similarly equipped.

SPECIFICATIONS

TYPE: *Two-seat dive-bomber/attack aircraft*

POWERPLANT: *One 1051 kW (1,410 hp) Junkers Jumo 211J-1 12-cylinder inverted Vee piston engine*

PERFORMANCE: *Maximum speed: 410 km/h (254 mph) at 3840 m (12,600 ft); Range: 1535 km (950 miles); Service ceiling: 7290 m (23,910 ft)*

WEIGHTS: *Empty: 3900 kg (8,580 lb); maximum take-off: 6600 kg (14,520 lb)*

ARMAMENT: *Two 37 mm (1.46 in) cannon in underwing gondolas and two 7.92 mm MG 81Z guns in rear cockpit*

DIMENSIONS: *Span: 13.80 m (45 ft); Length: 11.50 m (38 ft); Height: 3.90 m (13 ft); Wing area: 31.90 m² (343 sq ft)*

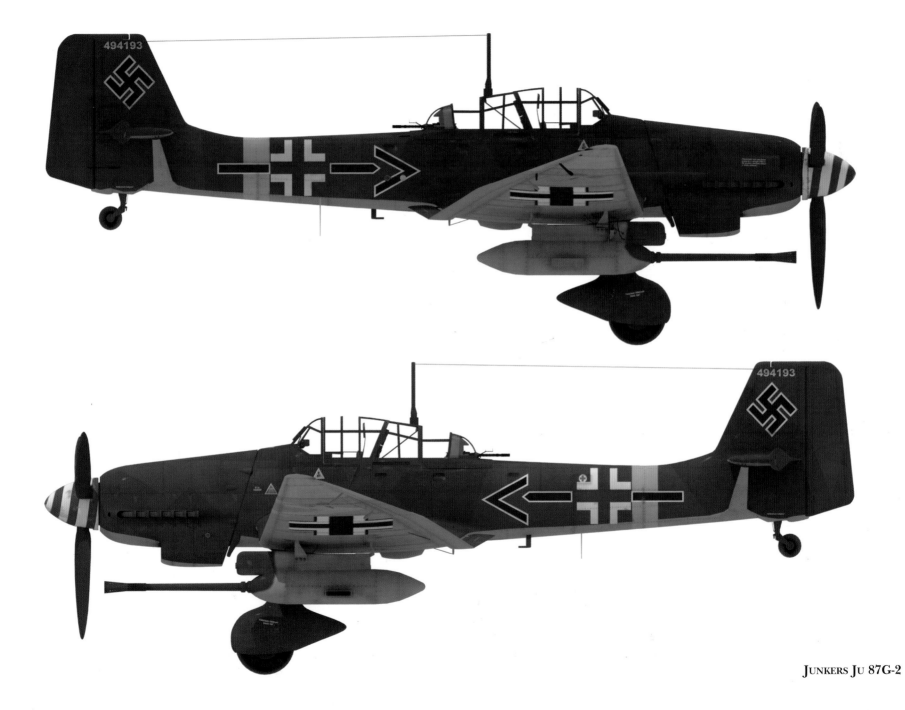

Junkers Ju 87G-2

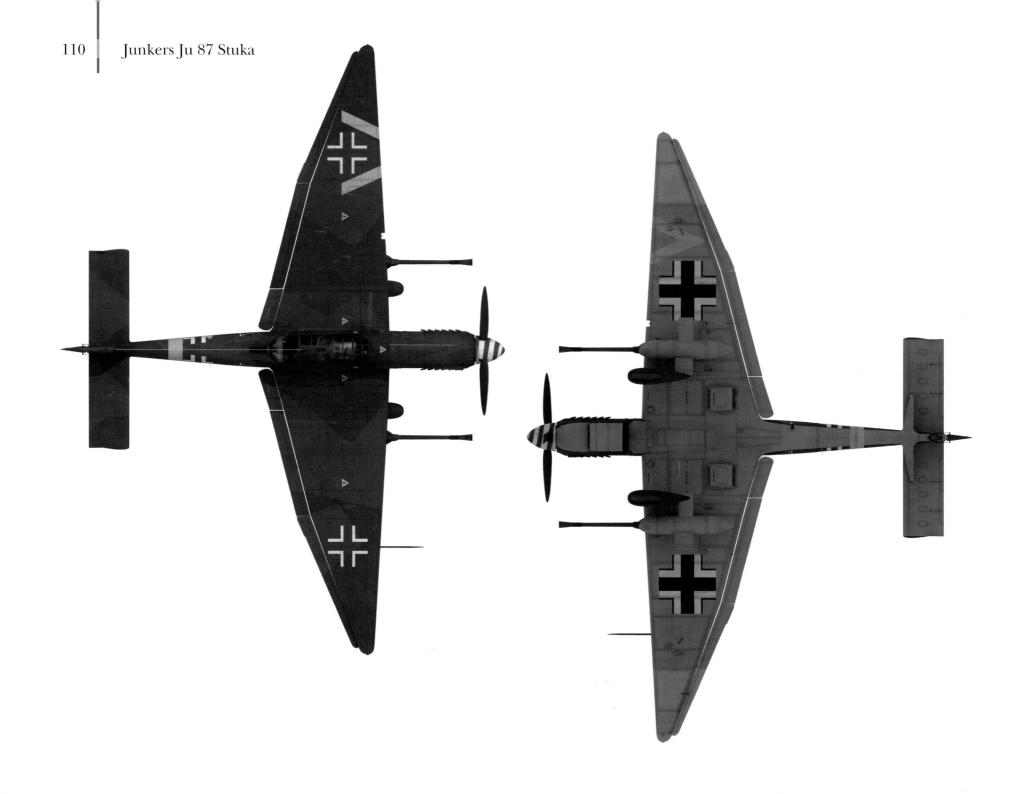

Tankbuster Supreme
A Ju 87G-2 of Major Hans-Ulrich Rudel's III Gruppe, Stukageschwader 2. In the course of German operations on the Eastern Front, Rudel destroyed 531 Soviet tanks and flew more than 2400 missions.

LONG-RANGE ATTACKER

The long-range Ju 87R version of the Stuka carried auxiliary fuel tanks under its wings, as seen here. It was used primarily for anti-shipping operations and was the final production variant to be based in the B-series airframe. The Ju 87R, known as the 'Richard', was first used against Royal Navy warships during the Norwegian campaign, and later saw extensive service in the Mediterranean and Russia.

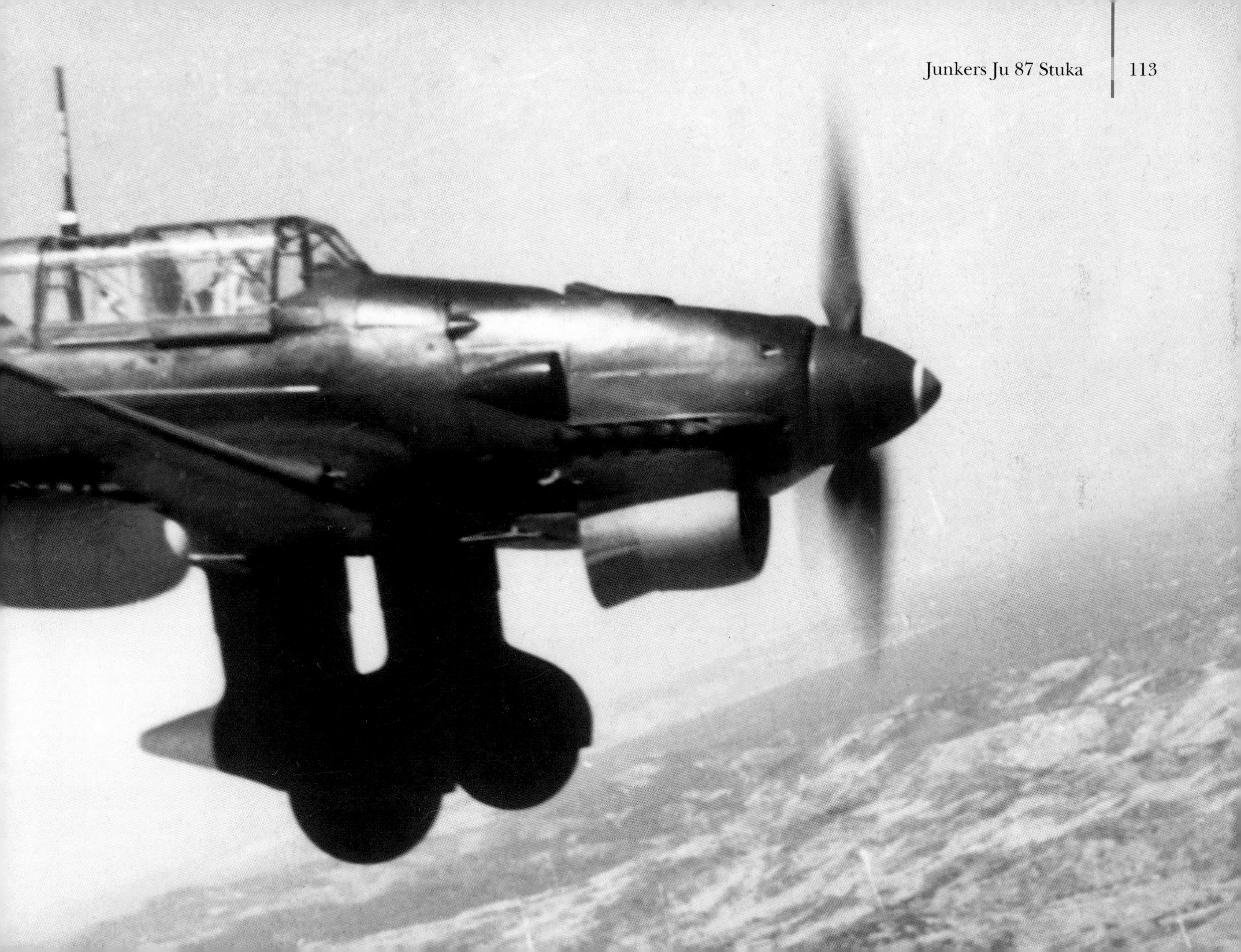

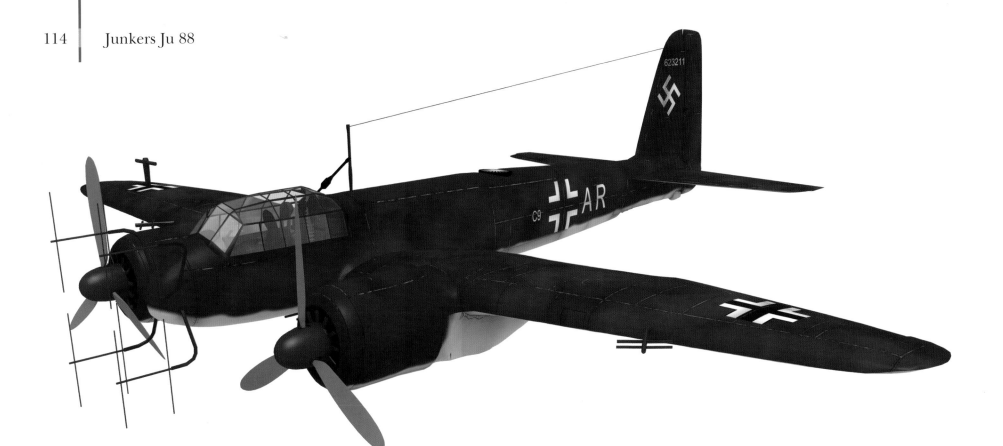

Junkers Ju 88

The versatile and effective Junkers Ju 88 was vitally important to the Luftwaffe during World War II, serving as bomber, dive-bomber, night fighter, close support aircraft, long-range heavy fighter, reconnaissance aircraft and torpedo-bomber. The most widely used variant was the Ju 88A-4, which served in both Europe and North Africa. The next major production model was the Ju 88C heavy fighter; the first version was the Ju 88C-2, a conversion of the Ju 88A-1 with a 'solid' nose housing three MG 17 machine guns and a 20 mm (0.79 in) MG FF cannon, plus a single rearward-firing MG 15. Entering service with NJG.1 in the late summer of 1940, it was used for intruder operations over the British Isles.

- The Ju 88 carried out its first operational mission – an attack on British warships in Scotland's Firth of Forth – in September 1939.
- The Ju 88A's most outstanding service was in the Arctic, where aircraft of KG 26 and KG 30, based in northern Norway, carried out devastating attacks on Allied convoys to Russia.
- The last fighter variant of the Ju 88, which made its appearance in the spring of 1944, was the Ju 88G. This version, which carried improved Lichtenstein AI radar, was a highly effective night fighter.

SPECIFICATIONS

TYPE: *Night fighter*

POWERPLANT: *Two 1250 kW (1,677 hp) BMW 801G radial engines*

PERFORMANCE: *Maximum speed: 550 km/h (342 mph); Range: 2500 km (1,553 miles); Service ceiling: 9900 m (32,480 ft)*

WEIGHTS: *Empty: 9081 kg (20,020 lb); Loaded: 13,100 kg (28,880 lb)*

ARMAMENT: *Four 20 mm (0.79 in) MG 151; one or two 13mm (0.5 in) MG 131 machine guns,*

DIMENSIONS: *Span: 20.08 m (65 ft 10 in); Length: 15.50 m (50 ft 10 in); Height: 5.07 m (16 ft 7 in); Wing area: 54.70 m² (587 sq ft)*

Junkers Ju 88G

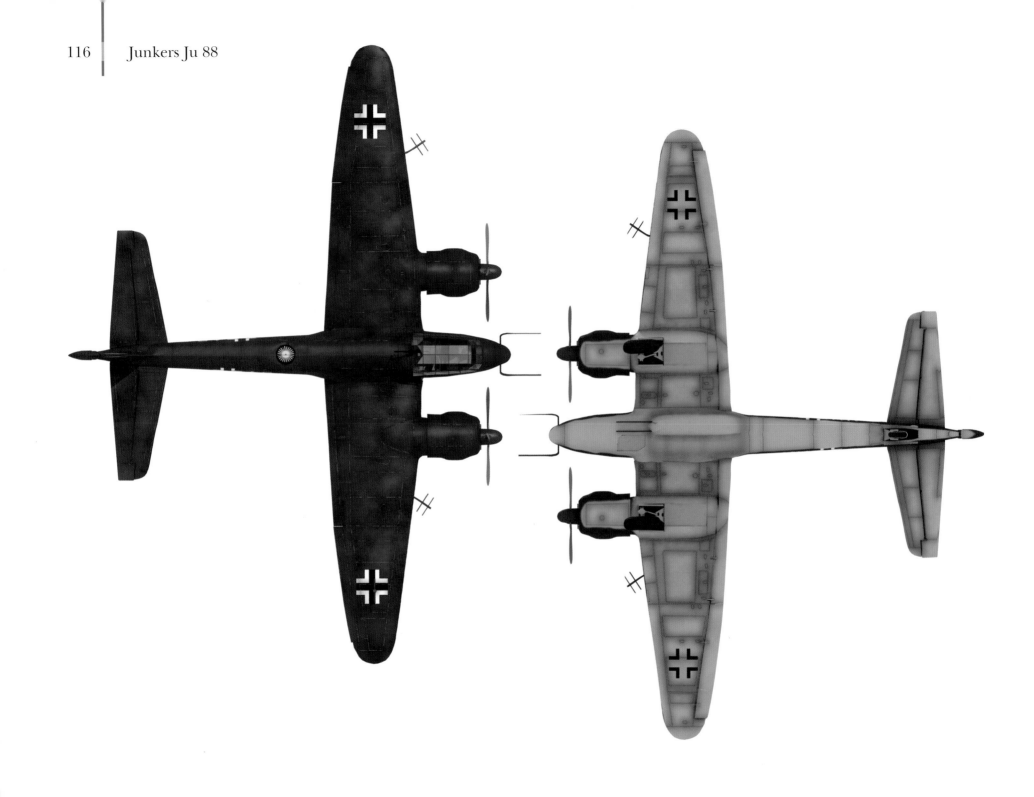

Potent Night Fighter
The code letters 'C9' on the fuselage of this Ju 88G night fighter reveal that it belongs to Nachtjagdgeschwader 5. The 'toasting fork' radar array on the nose is the antenna of the aircraft's Lichtenstein SN-2 airborne interception radar.

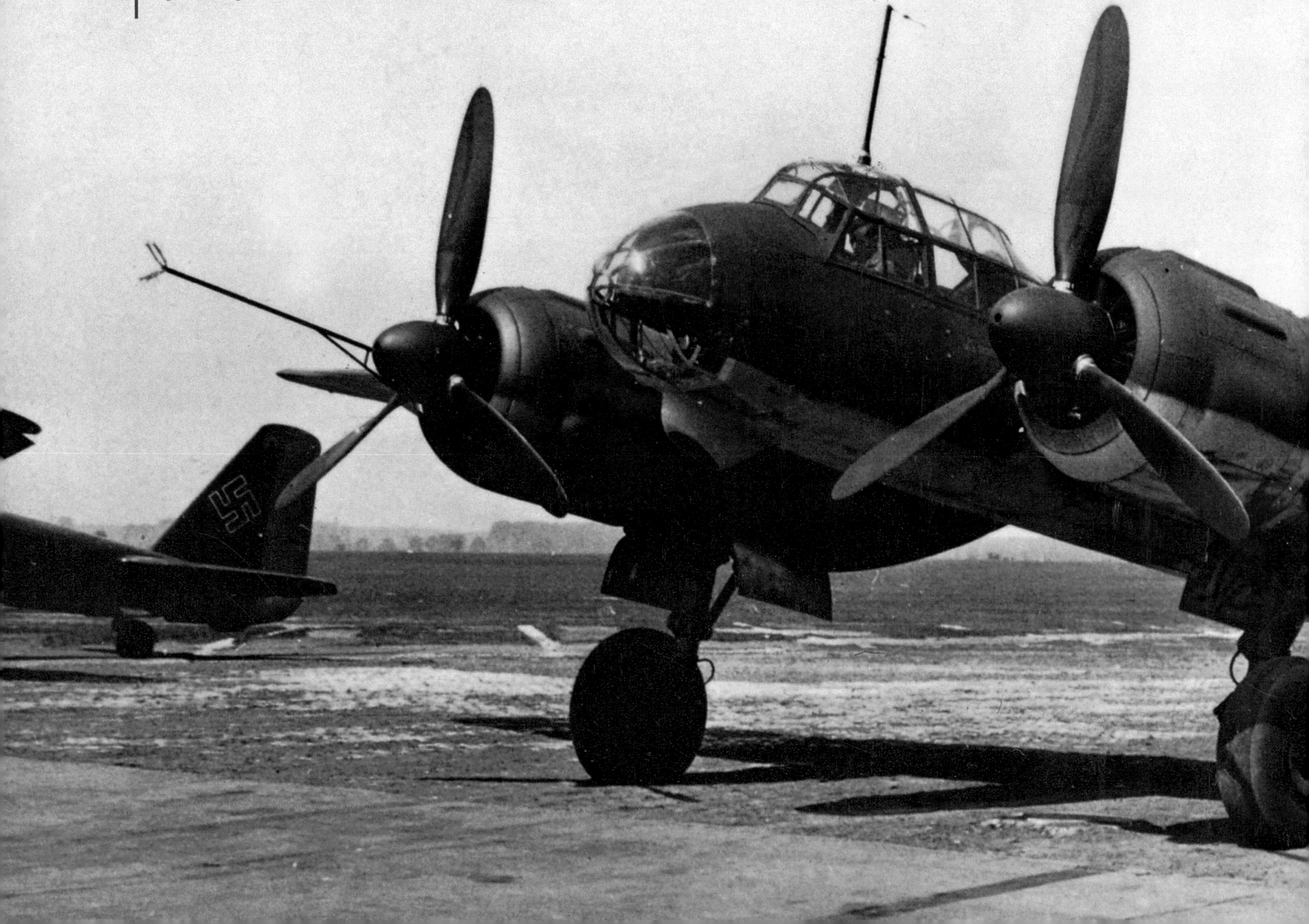

EFFECTIVE LAYOUT

The Junkers Ju 88's cockpit layout was better than that of other contemporary German bombers. The pilot sat in the front of the glazed cockpit, offset to port, with the navigator/bombardier seated on his right and slightly below him. The bombardier had easy access to the glazed nose section, where a bombsight was located for conventional bombing. For dive-bombing, the pilot used a sight mounted in the cockpit, which swung to the side when not in use. The flight engineer had the secondary task of operating the rearward-firing 7.92 mm (0.31 in) MG 15 machine gun in the rear of the glazed cabin. The Ju 88 was originally designed in response to a German Air Ministry requirement for a fast bomber; the dive-bombing capability was added later and was applied to all new German bombers.

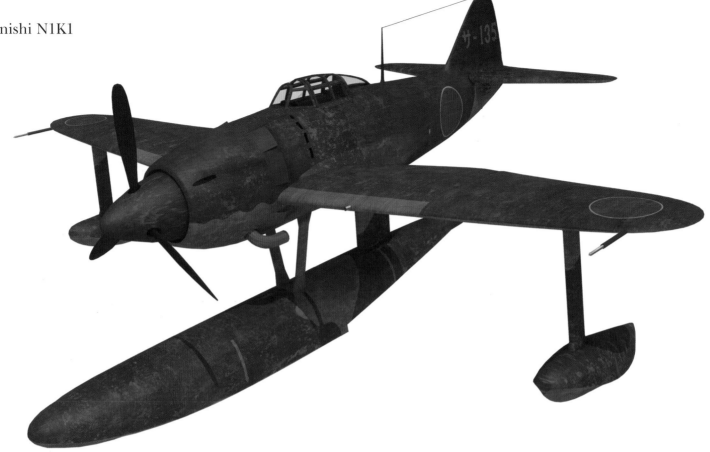

Kawanishi N1K1

A first-class design with excellent performance, the Kawanishi N1K Kyofu (Mighty Wind) made its appearance in the Pacific theatre in August 1942. Within three months, the decision was taken to convert the basic design to a landplane fighter configuration. Only 89 examples of the N1K-1 floatplane fighter were built; survivors were used in defence of the Japanese homeland in the last months of the war. The land-based fighter developed from the Kyofu fighter floatplane was the N1K-J Shiden (Violet Lightning); its production began in August 1943. One of the finest fighter aircraft to serve in the Pacific theatre, it was produced in two operational models, the N1K1-J and the N1K2-J model 21.

- The N1K2-J model 21 of the Shiden had a redesigned airframe that had its wing lowered from the mid-fuselage point to the lower fuselage and featured modified tail surfaces.
- The decision to end production of the floatplane version of the N1K1 in 1944 was a clear sign that Japan was now on the defensive and that the Imperial Japanese Navy no longer had any requirement for a floatplane fighter to support further offensive operations.
- The ending of Kyofu production also halted development of an advanced floatplane version, the N1K2.

SPECIFICATIONS

TYPE: *Floatplane fighter*

POWERPLANT: *One 1,480 kW (1,990 hp) Nakajima Homare NK9H radial engine*

PERFORMANCE: *Maximum speed: 594 km/h (369 mph); Range: 2,395 km (1,488 miles); Service ceiling: 10,800 m (35,500 ft)*

WEIGHTS: *Empty: 2,656 kg (5,855 lb); Loaded: 4,000 kg (8,820 lb)*

ARMAMENT: *Four 20 mm (0.79 in) Type 99 Model 2 Mk 4 cannon; 500 kg (1102 lb) of bombs*

DIMENSIONS: *Span: 12.0 m (39 ft 4 in); Length: 9.3 m (30 ft 7 in); Height: 3.9 m (13 ft 0 in); Wing area: 23.5 m² (253 sq ft)*

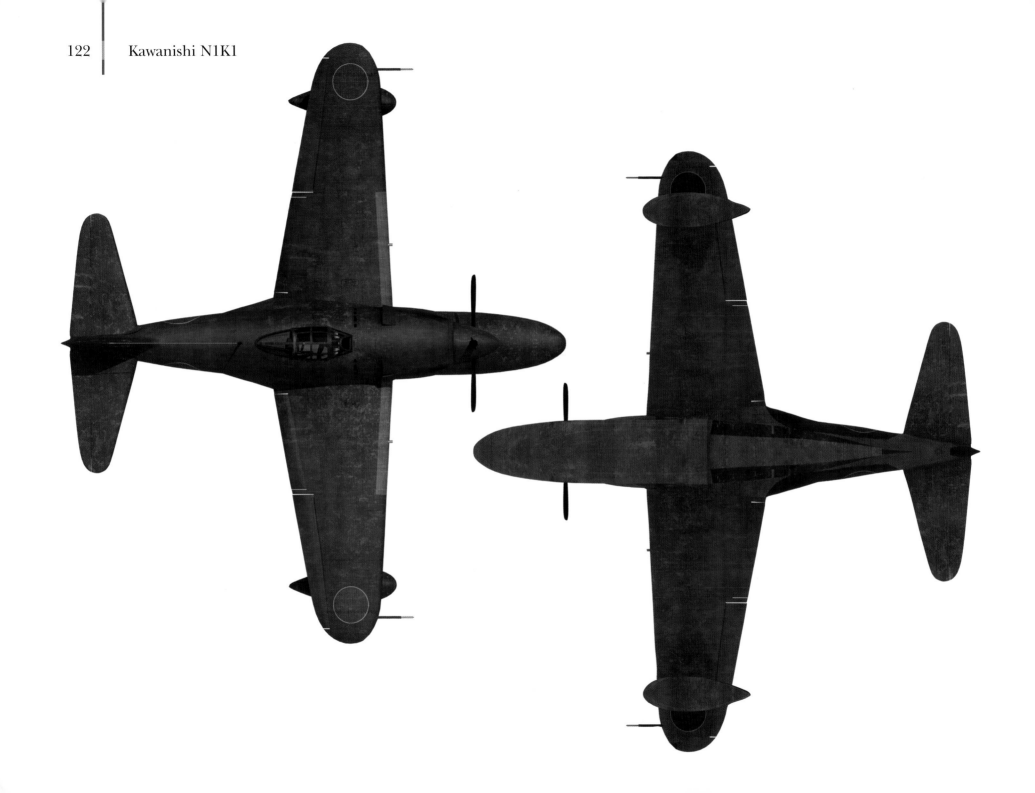

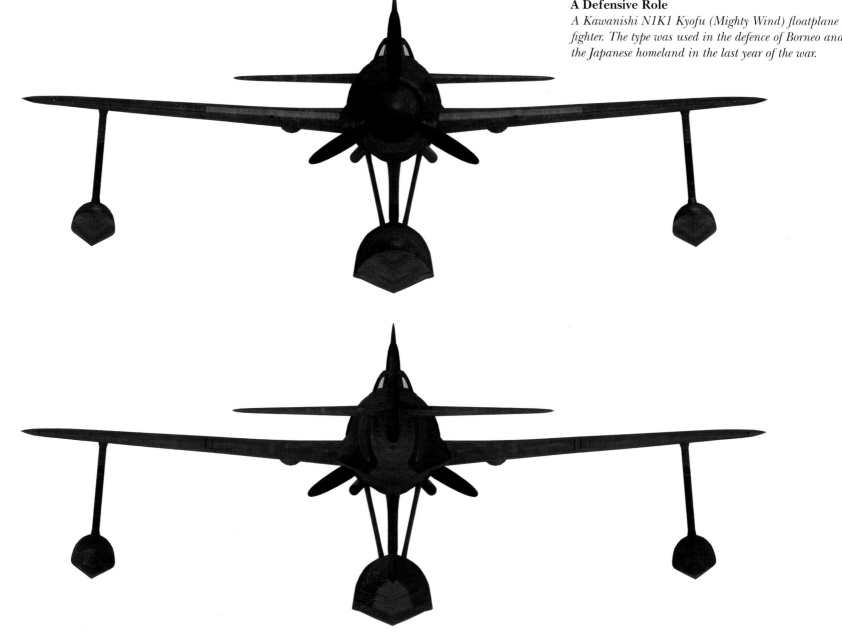

A Defensive Role
A Kawanishi N1K1 Kyofu (Mighty Wind) floatplane fighter. The type was used in the defence of Borneo and the Japanese homeland in the last year of the war.

SURPRISINGLY AGILE

Despite its large float, the Kawanishi N1K1 was fast and manoeuvrable. It shared the fighter floatplane task with the Nakajima A6M2-N, which was a floatplane fighter adaptation of the Mitsubishi A6M Zero and which was allocated the Allied codename 'Rufe'. The concept of the floatplane fighter, designed to operate from forward bases in the Pacific, was sound enough. As the war progressed, however, the problem of supplying such bases became acute, hence the decision to withdraw the floatplanes to bases within the rapidly shrinking defensive perimeter around the Japanese home islands. Before that, fighter floatplanes were often encountered by long-range Liberator bombers attacking targets in Burma from bases across the Bay of Bengal, and presented a significant threat.

Lockheed P-38 Lightning

It may have been overshadowed by the Republic P-47 Thunderbolt and the North American P-51 Mustang, but the Lockheed P-38 Lightning played a vital part in winning air superiority for the Allies, particularly in the Pacific theatre. The P-38 carried out many notable missions during World War II. Perhaps the most famous took place on 18 April 1943, when P-38 pilots of the 339th Fighter Squadron pulled off a spectacular coup. Flying to the limit of their combat radius from Guadalcanal, they shot down a G4M Betty bomber carrying Admiral Isoroku Yamamoto, Commander in Chief of the Japanese Combined Fleet and architect of the attack on Pearl Harbor. Leading German pilots, however, did not consider the type to be a formidable combat adversary. German ace Heinz Bar, who destroyed 16 enemy aircraft, had this to say about the P-38: 'Combat against American and British fighters was a highly varied thing, and pilot quality was the great imponderable factor until combat was actually joined. In general, P-38 Lightnings were not difficult at all. They were easy to outmanoeuvre and generally a sure victory.'

● Several variants of the P-38 were produced, the largest production run being achieved by the P-38L, which was fitted with a glazed nose and used as a bomber.
● The two top-scoring US pilots of the Pacific war, Majors Richard I Bong and Tommy McGuire, flew P-38s.
● The Lightning's twin tail booms were the type's distinctive recognition feature, and in the European theatre this led the Germans to nickname it the 'Gabelschwanzteufel', or 'Fork-Tailed Devil'.

SPECIFICATIONS

TYPE: *Single-seat fighter and fighter-bomber*

POWERPLANT: *Two turbo-charged 1194 kW (1,600 hp) Allison V-1710-111/113 in-line piston engines*

PERFORMANCE: *Maximum speed: 666 km/h (414 mph) at 7620 m (25,000 ft); Range: 765 km (475 miles) on internal fuel; Service ceiling: 13,400 m (44,000 ft)*

WEIGHTS: *Empty: 5806 kg (12,800 lb); Loaded: 9798 kg (21,600 lb)*

ARMAMENT: *One 20 mm (0.79 in) cannon and four 12.7 mm (.50 cal.) machine guns, plus up to 1450 kg (3,197 lb) of ordnance, usually two 454 kg (1,000 lb) or 726 kg (1,600 lb) bombs or 10 127 mm (5 in) rocket projectiles under wings*

DIMENSIONS: *Span: 15.85 m (52 ft); Length: 11.53 m (37 ft 10 in); Height: 3.00 m (9 ft 10 in); Wing area: 30.42 m² (327 sq ft)*

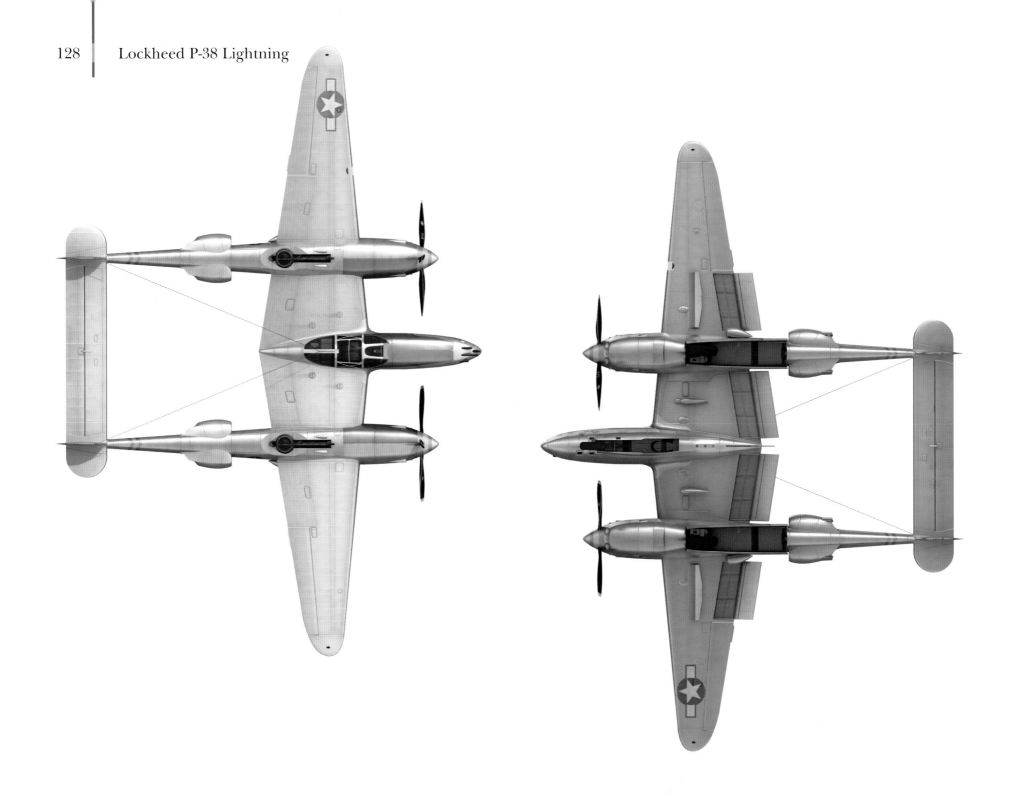

In Expert Hands
A P-38J Lightning of the 475th Fighter Group, to which top-scoring ace Major Tommy McGuire belonged. McGuire destroyed 38 Japanese aircraft before being killed in January 1944. He was awarded a posthumous Medal of Honor.

SUPERCHARGED

From the raised cockpit of the Lockheed P-38, the pilot had an excellent view forward, unobstructed by a propeller. The canopy hinged backwards and had downward-winding side windows. The P-38 Lightning had supercharged engines. In the early part of the war, the RAF wanted to buy substantial numbers of P-38s (in fact, it was the British who bestowed the name Lightning on the type); however, orders were cancelled when the Americans refused to fit the superchargers, which were deemed to be secret. This is a test aircraft in British markings, pictured in 1942.

Messerschmitt Bf 109

Like Britain's Hurricane and Spitfire, the Messerschmitt Bf 109 was developed in response to a 1933 requirement for a new monoplane fighter. Three Bf 109 prototypes were evaluated in Spain in February and March 1937, and were followed by 24 Bf 109B-2s, which immediately proved superior to any other fighter engaged in the civil war. This experience gave the Luftwaffe the tactical expertise that enabled it to wreak havoc among its opponents in the early years of World War II. By the war's outbreak, 1060 Bf 109s of various subspecies served with the Luftwaffe's fighter units. These included the Bf 109C and Bf 109D, which were already being replaced by the Bf 109E series. The Bf 109F began to reach Luftwaffe units in France in May 1941 and was superior in most respects to the principal RAF fighter of the time, the Spitfire Mk V. It was succeeded late in 1942 by the Bf 109G. The Bf 109G was built in Spain as the Hispano Ha 1109 and in Czechoslovakia as the Avia S-199. The last operational version of the Bf 109 was the 109K.

- The Bf 109E was the mainstay of the Luftwaffe's fighter units throughout 1940.
- The Bf 109F differed from the Bf 109E in having a generally cleaned-up airframe, redesigned engine cowling, wing, radiators and tail assembly.
- In all, Bf 109 production reached a total of about 35,000 aircraft.

SPECIFICATIONS

TYPE: *Single-seat fighter*

POWERPLANT: *One 876 kW (1,175 hp) Daimler-Benz DB 601A liquid-cooled inverted V-12 engine*

PERFORMANCE: *Maximum speed: 560 km/h (347 mph) at 4440 m (14,500 ft); Range: 660 km (410 miles); Service ceiling: 10,500 m (34,400 ft)*

WEIGHTS: *Empty: 1900 kg (4,180 lb); Maximum take-off: 2665 kg (5,863 lb)*

ARMAMENT: *One engine-mounted 20 mm (0.79 in) MG FF cannon and four 7.9 mm (0.31 in) MG 17 machine guns*

DIMENSIONS: *Span: 9.87 m (32 ft 4 in); Length: 8.64 m (28 ft 4 in); Height: 2.50 m (8 ft 3 in); Wing area: 16.40 m² (176 sq ft)*

MESSERSCHMITT BF 109E-4

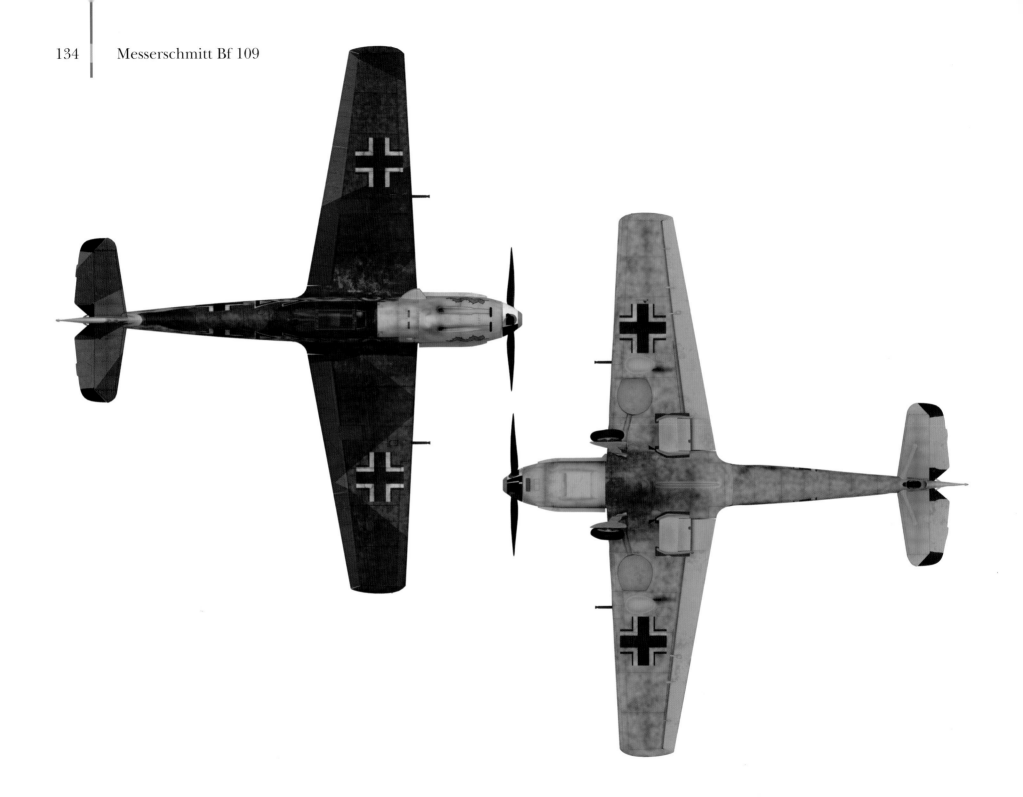

Fearsome Foe
This Messerschmitt Bf 109E-4 of 1/JG 3 was flown by Leutnant Hans von Hahn, the unit's Gruppenkammandeur, in the autumn of 1940. Note the 'Tatzelwurm' (clawed serpent) insignia on the engine cowling.

ACCIDENT ATTRITION

Professor Willi Messerschmitt had originally intended the Bf 109's thin, frail wings to be left free of guns. When the Luftwaffe High Command learned that the Spitfire and Hurricane were to be fitted with eight machine guns, however, they insisted that the Bf 109 was to carry wing-mounted guns too. Messerschmitt was therefore forced to design a new wing, with bulges for the ammunition boxes of the 20 mm (0.79 in) cannon mounted on each side. One innovation, the Bf 109's narrow-track undercarriage, was designed so that the fuselage rather than the wings bore the weight of the aircraft on the ground; however, five per cent of all 109s built, some 1750 aircraft in total, were destroyed in landing accidents.

Messerschmitt Bf 110

Designed as a long-range escort fighter, the twin-engine Messerschmitt Bf 110 was not a success story in its intended role – it could be outmanoeuvred by both the Spitfire and Hurricane. Losses in the Battle of Britain were heavy, but despite this the aircraft remained in production for some time, mainly because the Me 129, which was to have replaced it, was a failure. Later in the war, however, the Bf 110 proved its worth as a night fighter. In July 1941, a prototype German Lichtenstein airborne interception (AI) radar set was installed in a Bf 110 at Leeuwarden, Holland. On 9 August, this aircraft successfully intercepted and shot down a Wellington bomber. Escort fighter variants of the Bf 110 were originally designed to carry a crew of three: pilot, radio operator and gunner. In practice a crew of two was usually carried, the radio operator also acting as the gunner. The Bf 110C-4 was the first variant to introduce armour protection for the crew.

- The Bf 110 carried four 7.92 mm (0.31 in) machine guns in the upper nose, staggered so that they fitted into the narrow fuselage.
- Two MG FF 20 mm (0.79 in) cannon were mounted in the lower fuselage beneath the pilot's seat. The gunner was armed with a single .92 mm (0.31 in) MG 15 machine gun with 750 rounds of ammunition.
- The hood on the gunner's section of the cockpit could be swung upwards to give a better field of fire.

SPECIFICATIONS

TYPE: *Two-seat fighter-bomber/reconnaissance fighter*

POWERPLANT: *Two 895 kW (1,200 hp) Daimler-Benz DB 601N inverted V-12 piston engines*

PERFORMANCE: *Maximum speed: 562 km/h (348 mph) at 7000 m (22,960 ft); Range: 850 km (527 miles); Service ceiling: 10,000 m (33,000 ft)*

WEIGHTS: *Empty: 4500 kg (9,900 lb); Loaded: 7000 kg (15,400 lb)*

ARMAMENT: *Two 20 mm (0.79 in) Oerlikon MG FF cannon in belly and four 7.92 mm (0.31 in) MG 17 machine guns in nose; one 7.92 mm MG 15 machine gun in rear cockpit; racks for four 250 kg (550 lb) bombs under centre section*

DIMENSIONS: *Span: 16.25 m (53 ft); Length: 12.10 m (40 ft); Height: 3.50 m (11 ft); Wing area: 39.40 m² (424 sq ft)*

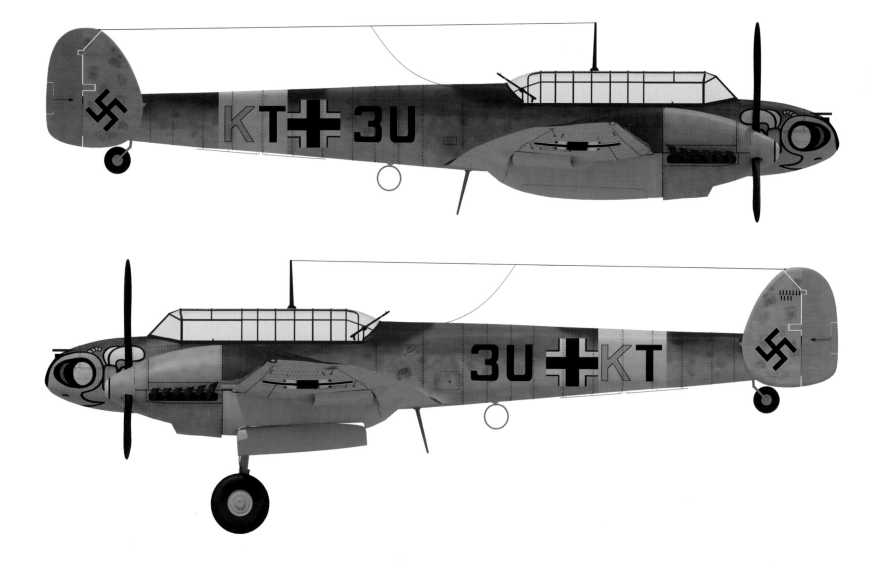

MESSERSCHMITT BF 110C

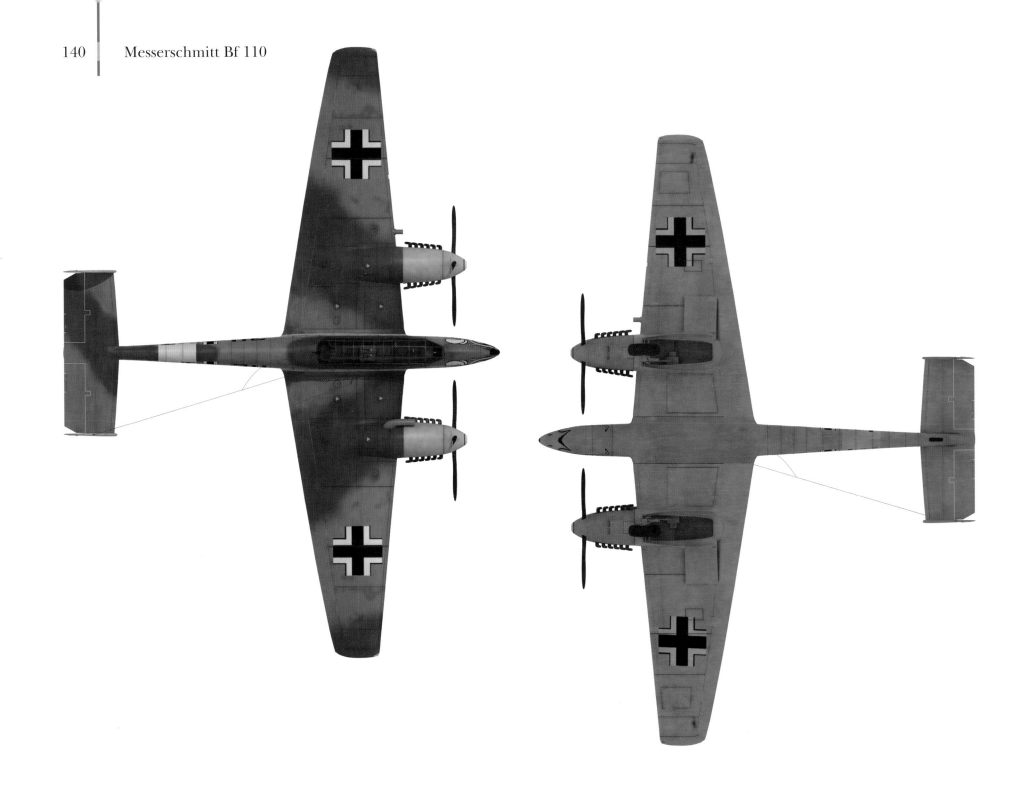

Desert Colours

The code markings indicate that this is a Messerschmitt Bf 110C of Zerstorergeschwader (ZG) 26 'Horst Wessel', a unit that suffered particularly heavy losses in the Battle of Britain. The aircraft is seen in desert camouflage, applied when ZG 26 deployed to the Mediterranean theatre.

EARLY SUCCESS

In the early months of World War II, exponents of the Bf 110 were encouraged by the aircraft's success against RAF bombers, mainly Handley Page Hampdens, operating in daylight over the North Sea in search of enemy shipping. Two Bf 110s would position themselves abeam the Hampden, one off each of the bomber's wingtips, and their gunners would open fire. The Hampden's gunner was unable to retaliate as his machine gun, intended to defend against attacks from astern, had a restricted arc of fire and he could not bring it to bear on the Messerschmitts.

Messerschmitt Me 163 Komet

The remarkable and revolutionary Me 163 rocket-powered interceptor was yet another example of German ingenuity, but came too late to alter the course of the air war. Based on the experimental DFS 194, the first two Me 163 prototypes were flown in the spring of 1941 as unpowered gliders. The Me 163V-1 was transferred to Peenemunde later in the year to be fitted with its 7.3 kN (1653 lb thrust) Walter HWK R.II rocket motor. In May 1944, after operational trials with Erprobungkommando EK 16, whose principal function was to pioneer the Me 163B (the fully operational version) into Luftwaffe use, and to train a cadre of experienced pilots, an operational Komet unit, JG400, began forming at Wittmundhaven and Venlo. In June, all three Staffeln of this unit moved to Brandis near Leipzig, together with EK16.

- The first rocket-powered flight was made in August 1941, and during subsequent trials the Me 163 broke all existing world air speed records, reaching speeds of up to 1000 km/h (620 mph).
- The task of the Komets at Brandis was to defend the Leuna oil refinery, 90 km (55 miles) to the south.
- About 300 Komets were built, but JG400 remained the only operational unit, and the rocket fighter recorded only nine kills during its brief career.

SPECIFICATIONS

TYPE: *Single-seat rocket-powered interceptor*

POWERPLANT: *One 16.6 kN (3,748 lb thrust) Walter 109-509A-2 rocket motor*

PERFORMANCE: *Maximum speed: 955 km/h (593 mph); Range 35.5km (22 miles); Service ceiling 12,000 m (39,370 ft)*

WEIGHT: *Loaded: 4310 kg (9,502 lb)*

ARMAMENT: *two 30 mm (1.18 in) Mk 108 cannon in wing roots*

DIMENSIONS: *Span: 9.33 m (30 ft 7 in); Length: 5.85 m (19 ft 2 in); Height: 2.76 m (9 ft); Wing area: 18.5 m² (200 sq ft)*

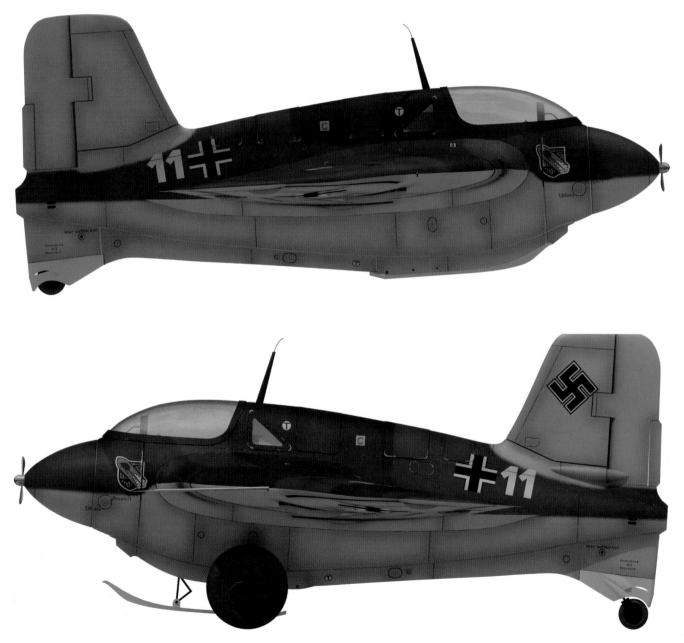

MESSERSCHMITT ME 163 KOMET

Explosive Landings

JG400 was the only operational unit to receive the Me 163. Seen here is an aircraft of 2 Staffel (2./JG 400). The Komet had a nasty tendency to explode on touchdown, and many pilots were lost in accidents.

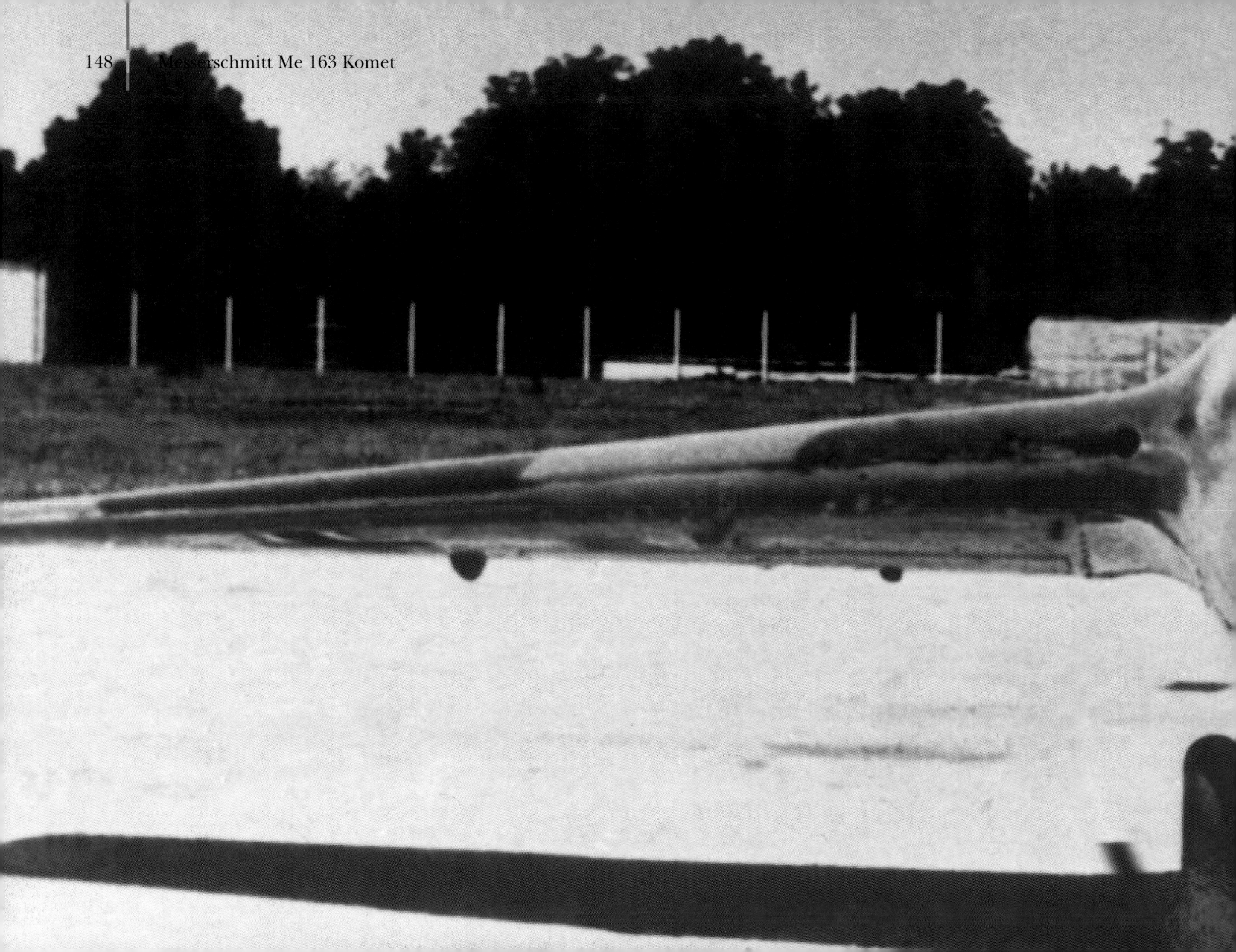

IMPRESSIVE STATISTICS

Taking off on its jettisonable trolley, the Komet would climb initially at 3600 m/min (11,800 ft/min), this rate rising to 10,200 m/min (33,470 ft/min) at 9760 m (32,800 ft). Time to the Komet's operational ceiling of 12,100 m (39,690 ft) was a mere 3.35 minutes. Maximum powered endurance was eight minutes. With its fuel exhausted, the Me 163 would make high-speed gliding attacks on its targets, using its two MK 108 30 mm (1.18 in) cannon and Revi 16B gunsight. With its 120 rounds of ammunition used up and its speed beginning to drop, the Komet would then dive steeply away from the combat area and glide back to base, landing on a skid. The Me 163C variant was to have been fitted with five vertically mounted tubes in each wing, each tube containing a 50 mm (1.97 in) shell. The equipment was activated by a photo-electric cell as the rocket fighter passed under an enemy bomber.

Messerschmitt Me 262

The Me 262 jet fighter presented a serious threat to Allied air superiority during World War II's closing months. Faster than any Allied fighter then in service, including Britain's Gloster Meteor jet, its main drawback was the unreliability of its turbojet engines, which had a life of only about 25 hours before they needed to be changed. It also suffered from the whims of Adolf Hitler, whose obsession with using the aircraft as a bomber led to a delay of six years between it taking shape on Messerschmitt's drawing board and its entry into Luftwaffe service. Despite its engine problems, the Me 162 was a superb aircraft.

- By the end of October 1944, an Me 262 fighter trials unit known as the Kommando Nowotny had reached operational status and was deployed to the airfields of Achmer and Hesepe near Osnabruck.
- Even though its base was astride the main US daylight bomber approach route, Kommando Nowotny was usually able to fly only three or four sorties a day against enemy formations because of technical problems and a lack of adequately trained pilots. Yet in November 1944 the Me 262s destroyed 22 aircraft.
- If the Me 162 had reached full operational status in the early months of 1944, it might have robbed the Allies of the air superiority they needed for the invasion of Europe.

SPECIFICATIONS

TYPE: *Single-seat air superiority fighter*

POWERPLANT: *Two 8.82-kN (1,980 lb-thrust) Junkers Jumo 004B-1, -2 or -3 axial-flow turbojets*

PERFORMANCE: *Maximum speed: 870 km/h (540 mph); Range: 1050 km (650 miles) at 9000 m (30,000 ft); Service ceiling: 11,450 m (37,500 ft)*

WEIGHTS: *Empty: 3800 kg (8,738 lb); Maximum take-off: 6400 kg (14,110 lb)*

ARMAMENT: *Four 30 mm (1.18 in) Rheinmetall-Borsig MK 108A-3 cannon;12 R4M air-to-air rockets; two 226 kg (500 lb) bombs or one 452 kg (1,000 lb) bomb*

DIMENSIONS: *Span: 12.50 m (40 ft 11 in); Length: 10.58 m (34 ft 9 in); Height: 3.83 m (12 ft 7 in); Wing area: 21.73 m² (234 sq ft)*

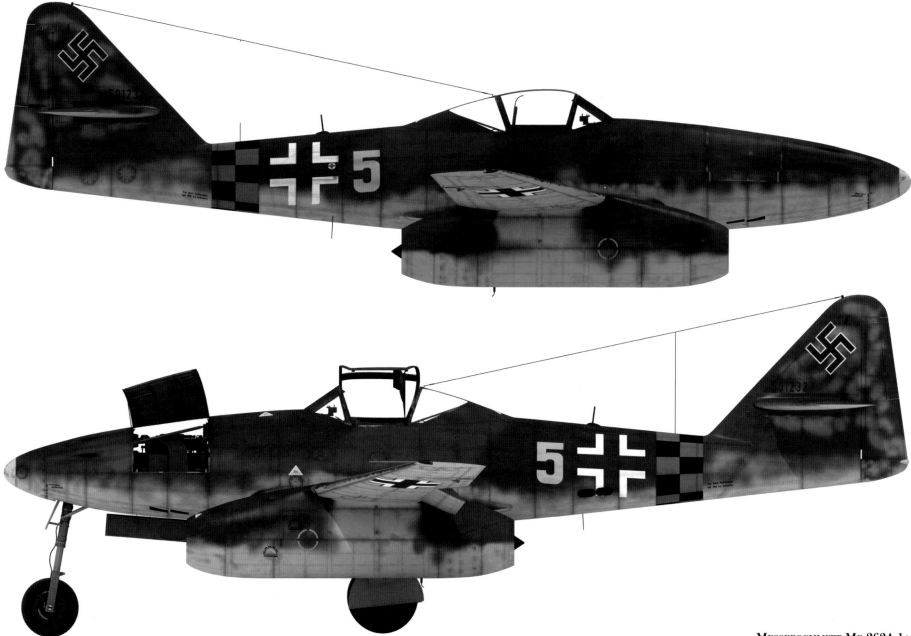

MESSERSCHMITT ME 262A-1A

Leading by Example
The first fully operational Me 262 fighter unit was Jagdgeschwader JG7 Hindenburg, one of whose aircraft is pictured here. It was commanded by Oberstleutnant Johannes Steinhoff, an ace who ended World War II with 176 victories.

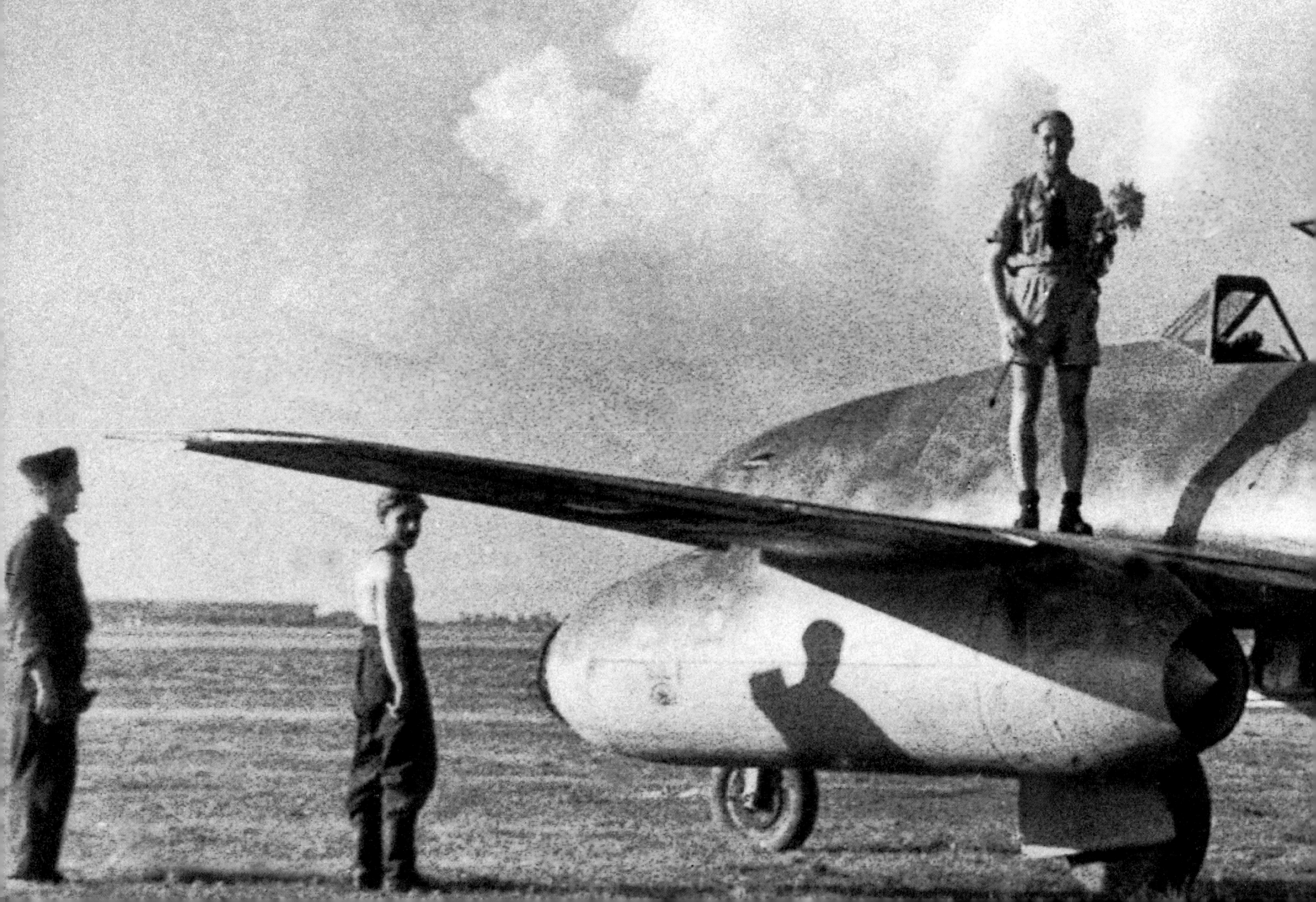

SCATTERSHOT TACTICS

In the middle of February 1945, III/JG 7 took delivery of the first consignment of R4M 50 mm (1.97 in) air-to-air rockets; the Me 262 could carry 24 of these missiles mounted on simple wooden racks beneath the wings. When the salvo was fired towards an enemy bomber formation, it spread out rather like the charge from a shotgun, increasing the chances of hitting one or more targets. During their first series of operations using a combination of R4Ms, 30 mm (1.18 in) cannon and Revi gunsight, in the last week of February 1945, the pilots of III/JG 7 destroyed no fewer than 45 four-engined American bombers and 15 of their escorting fighters for the loss of only four Me 262s.

Mitsubishi A6M2 Zero

The quality of Japanese aircraft came as an unpleasant surprise to the Allies at the outbreak of the Pacific war. This was embodied in one type: the Mitsubishi A6M Zero. One of the finest aircraft of all time, the Mitsubishi A6M Reisen (Zero fighter) first flew on 1 April 1939, and soon showed itself clearly superior to any fighter the Allies could put into the air in the Pacific war's early stages. Highly manoeuvrable and structurally very strong, despite being lightweight, it was constructed in two pieces, instead of being built in several separate units. It had no armour plating for the pilot and no self-sealing fuel tanks, however, and so was unable to absorb as much battle damage as Allied fighters. The Zero retained its overall ascendancy during the Pacific conflict's first year, despite the Japanese suffering some serious reverses over this time.

- The Zero's engine, cockpit and forward fuselage combined with the wings to form one rigid unit; the second unit comprised the rear fuselage and the tail. The two were joined together by a ring of 80 bolts.
- As World War II progressed, the Zero was outclassed by American fighters such as the Grumman F6F Wildcat and Vought Corsair.
- In the war's latter months, many Zeros were fitted with bombs and expended in kamikaze suicide attacks.

SPECIFICATIONS

Type: *Single-seat carrier-based fighter-bomber*

Powerplant: *One 843 kW (1,130 hp) Nakajima NK1F Sakae 21 radial engine*

Performance: *Maximum speed: 565 km/h (350 mph); Range: 1800km (1,200 miles) with drop-tank; Service ceiling: 11,740 m (38,500 ft)*

Weights: *Empty: 1876 kg (4,000 lb); Loaded: 2733 kg (6,025 lb)*

Armament: *Two 7.7 mm (.303 cal.) machine guns with 600 rounds above the engine and two 20 mm (0.79 in) Type 99 cannon with 100 rounds each in the wings, plus two 60 kg (130 lb) bombs under wings (or one 250 kg/550 lb bomb)*

Dimensions: *Span: 11.00 m (36 ft 1 in); Length: 9.12 m (29 ft 11 in); Height: 3.60 m (11 ft 6 in); Wing area: 21.30 m² (230 sq ft)*

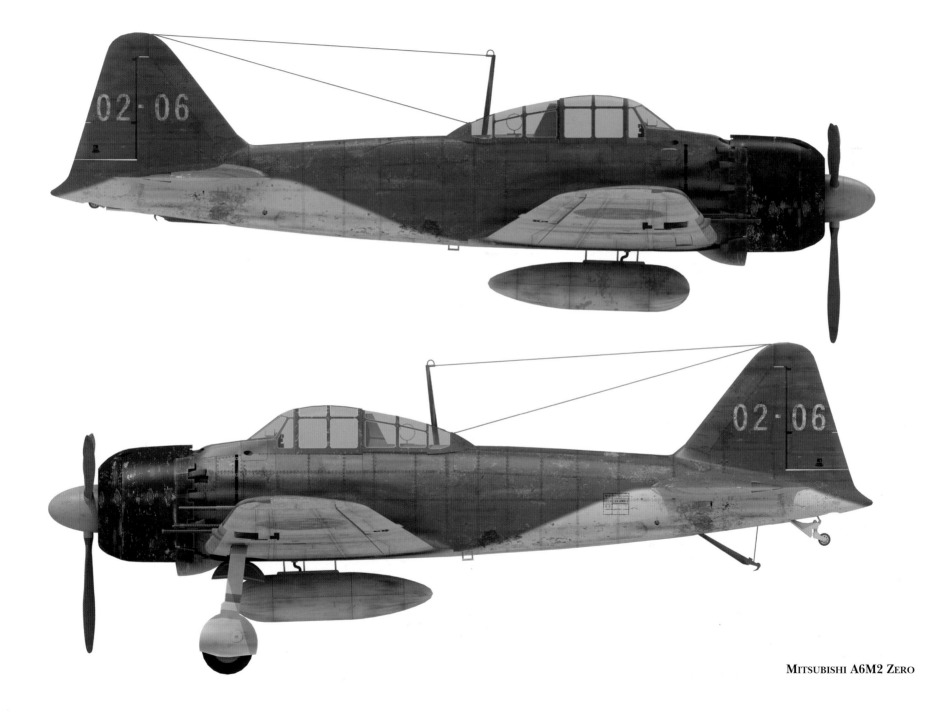

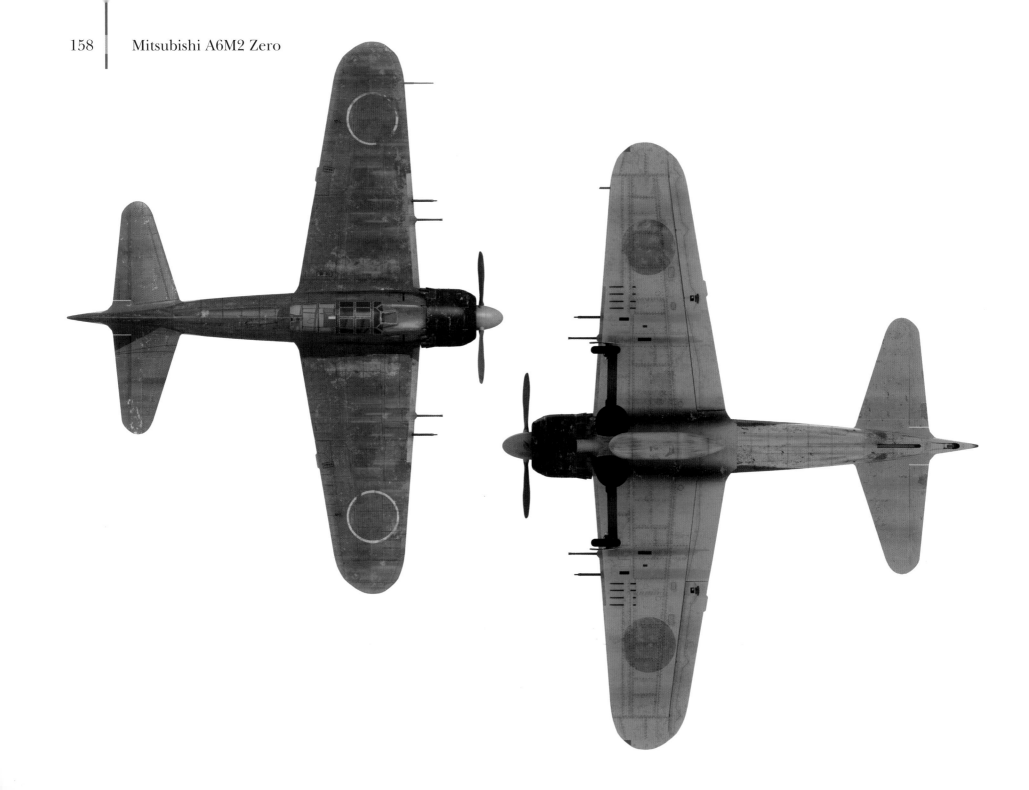

Naval Flyer
A Mitsubishi A6M2 Zero of the Oiku Kokutai (Naval Air Corps). The Kokutai was the basic air unit of the Imperial Japanese Navy, and each one had a strength of about 150 aircraft.

EKING OUT ENDURANCE

Although the Mitsubishi Zero presented some serious drawbacks in combat, the greatest of which was its inability to absorb punishment because of its lack of self-sealing fuel tanks and armour plating, its greatest assets were its manoeuvrability and its long range. All Imperial Japanese Navy pilots practised long-range flying and were skilled at coaxing the best possible endurance out of their aircraft, which was vital when operating over the vast expanse of the Pacific Ocean. In the early days of the Pacific war, Allied pilots who took off to intercept Japanese bombers were shocked to find the latter strongly escorted by Zero fighters, operating at extreme range. At this early stage, Japanese pilots did not carry parachutes, which helped to save weight.

Mitsubishi G4M 'Betty'

The Imperial Japanese Navy's standard medium bomber of the late 1930s was the Mitsubishi G3M, which saw widespread service in the Pacific war. The G3M had excellent performance, but the Japanese Naval Staff was anxious to make improvements with special regard to speed and range, and in the second half of 1937 Mitsubishi developed the G4M. The prototype first flew on 23 October 1939; initial production G4M1 versions came off the assembly lines from April 1941. In November 1942, the much-improved G4M2 made its appearance, and the G4M1 was assigned to transport, reconnaissance and training duties. The G4M lacked protective armour and self-sealing fuel tanks, making it very easy to shoot down. This was rectified in the last bomber version, the G4M3, but only 60 were completed out of a total figure of 2479.

- About 200 G4M1s were in service at the time of the attack on Pearl Harbor, and were used in the torpedo attack as well as the level-bombing role.
- The G4M, which received the Allied code name 'Betty', featured in all of Japan's Pacific campaigns, its range enabling it to carry out attacks on Darwin and other targets in northern Australia.
- One subvariant, the G4M2e, was specially modified to carry the Ohka piloted suicide aircraft.

SPECIFICATIONS

TYPE: *Twin-engined seven-seat land-based naval medium bomber*

POWERPLANT: *Two 1343 kW (1,800 hp) Mitsubishi Kasei 25 radial engines*

PERFORMANCE: *Maximum speed: 438 km/h (270 mph) at 4,600 m (15,000 ft); Range: 4335 km (2,694 miles)*

WEIGHTS: *Empty: 8160 kg (17,952 lb); Loaded: 12,500 kg (27,500 lb)*

ARMAMENT: *One 20 mm (0.79 in) cannon in tail, two 7.92 mm (0.31 in) machine guns in nose and one in beam position; 1000 kg (2,200 lb) of bombs or one 800 kg (1,760 lb) torpedo*

DIMENSIONS: *Span: 25.00 m (82 ft); Length: 20 m (66 ft); Height: 6 m (2 ft); Wing area: 78.12 m² (841 sq ft)*

Mitsubishi G4M 'Betty'

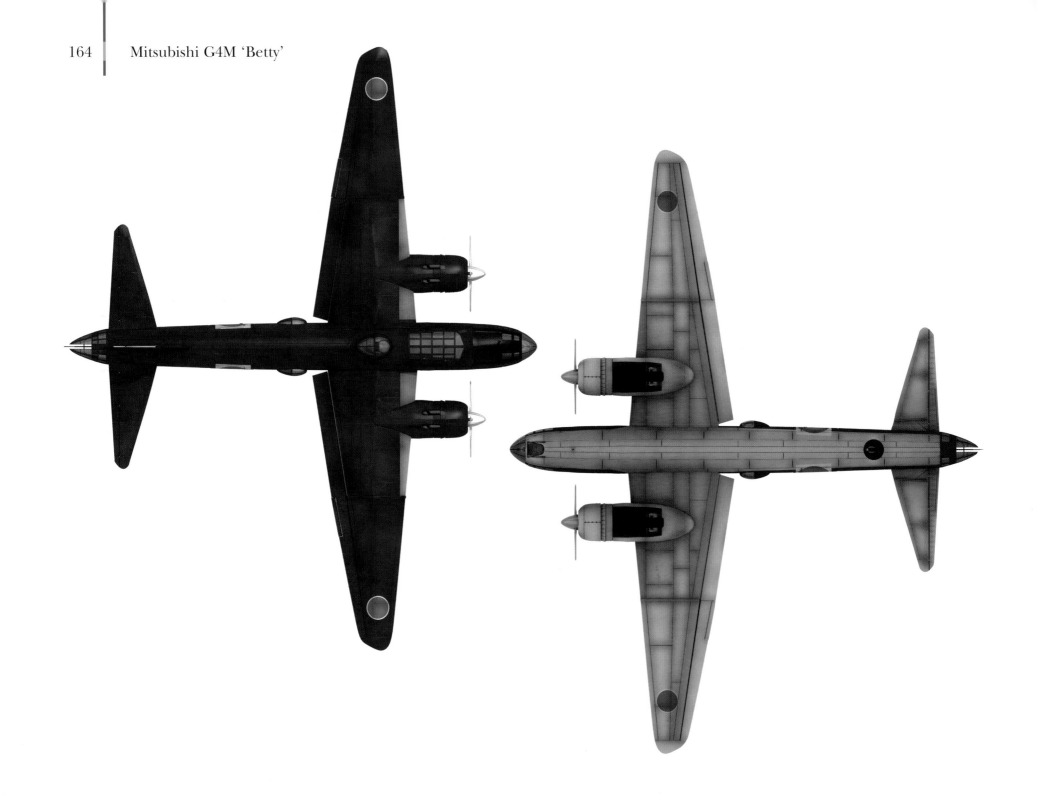

Aggression against China
A G4M Betty of the Japanese 705th Naval Air Corps. Nicknamed Hamaki (Cigar) by its crews because of the shape of its fuselage, the G4M flew its first operational missions against targets deep in mainland China in the summer of 1941.

TESTING THE 'BETTY'

A captured Mitsubishi G4M2a Navy Type 1 Attack Bomber 24, known as 'Betty' to the Allies, under test in the United States. Because of a lack of defensive armour, the Betty was never able to sustain any degree of battle damage and caught fire easily. The last units to use the G4M in action suffered terrible losses during Kamikaze operations in the final months of the Pacific War. The Ohka piloted suicide weapon it carried made the aircraft very heavy and slow, making it an easy target for Allied fighter aircraft.

Nakajima B5N

Designed in 1936, the prototype B5N torpedo-bomber first flew in January 1937 and became operational as the B5N1 light bomber in China. Most B5N-1s were allocated to a training role as they were progressively replaced by the B5N2 in 1939–40. B5N2s featured prominently in the Pearl Harbor attack, with 144 of them taking part in the strike. In the year that followed, B5N2s delivered fatal blows to the US aircraft carriers *Lexington*, *Yorktown* and *Hornet*, provided support for Japanese amphibious assaults and took part in a carrier strike on Ceylon, in which heavy damage was inflicted on installations in the port of Colombo. The B5N2 remained in production until 1943; in total, 1149 examples of both variants were built. Many B5Ns were later assigned to anti-submarine patrol work, a task eminently suited to their long endurance.

- The B5N was known to the Allies as 'Kate', and when the Pacific war began it was the most modern carrier-borne torpedo bomber in service with any of the world's navies.
- Operating in areas where Allied fighters were not usually active, B5Ns provided desperately needed air cover to Japanese maritime convoys, which were being decimated by prowling US submarines.
- Some B5Ns had Air to Surface Vessel (ASV) radar, with aerials fitted along the sides of the rear fuselage.

SPECIFICATIONS

TYPE: *Three-crew torpedo-bomber*

POWERPLANT: *One 843 kW (1,000 hp) Nakajima Sakae 11 radial engine*

PERFORMANCE: *Maximum speed: 367 km/h (229 mph); Range: 1,935 km (1,202 miles); Service ceiling: 8,260 m (27,100 ft)*

WEIGHTS: *Empty: 2,279 kg (5,024 lb); Loaded: 3,800 kg (8,380 lb)*

ARMAMENT: *One 7.7 mm Type 92 machine gun; One 800 kg (1,760 lb) Type 91 torpedo or 750 kg (1,653 lb) of bombs*

DIMENSIONS: *Span: 15.52 m (50 ft 11 in); Length: 10.30 m (33 ft 10 in); Height: 3.70 m (12 ft 2 in); Wing area: 37.7 m² (406 sq ft)*

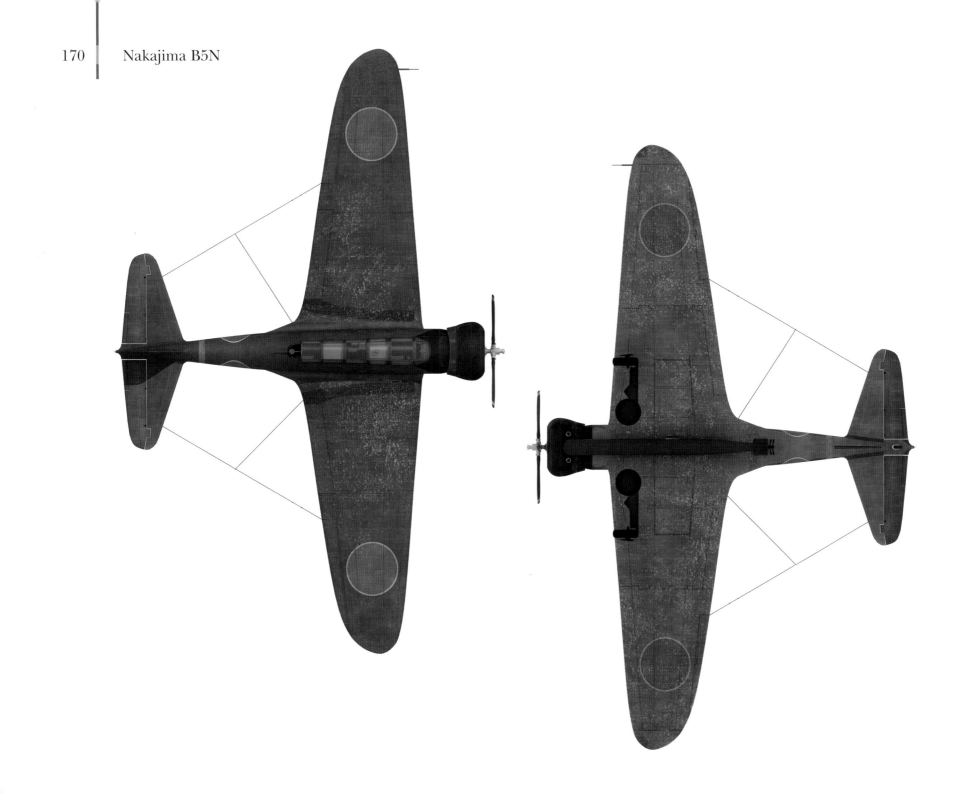

Tactical Bombing
The Nakajima B5N1, seen here, served as a land-based tactical bomber in China, operating in support of ground units and escorted by carrier-borne fighters. The type was quite successful in this role, despite being vulnerable to ground fire.

COMMON DRAWBACKS

A clean, low-wing design with a hydraulically operated retractable undercarriage, the Nakajima B5N incorporated a number of innovations. The large wing could be folded upwards, and the hinge points were so arranged that the wingtips overlapped each other when folded above the cockpit. Other refinements to the aicraft included Fowler flaps and a variable-pitch propeller, although the Fowler flaps, which extended when lowered to increase the wing area, were later replaced by more conventional units because of concerns that they would create maintenance problems. The B5N's main drawback, a feature it had in common with other Japanese types, was its lack of armour, self-sealing fuel tanks and defensive firepower. The latter was limited to a single machine gun.

Nakajima Ki-84 Hayate

A deadly fighter aircraft in the hands of an experienced pilot, the Nakajima Ki-84 Hayate (Gale) was one of the few entirely new fighters developed by the Japanese aircraft industry after the Pacific war's outbreak. An immensely potent fighting machine, it was undoubtedly Japan's best fighter of the war. It could climb faster and was more manoeuvrable than either the P-51D Mustang or P-47N Thunderbolt. Unfortunately for Japan, it came too late to stem the Allied air onslaught, which was gathering momentum in 1944. The Hayate – given the Allied code name 'Frank' – was designed as a replacement for the Nakajima Ki-44 Shoki (Demon), which was in widespread service with the Japanese Army Air Force. At the end of 1944, production of the Shoki was suspended, and the Hayate fighter was ordered into mass production.

● About 3500 examples of the Hayate were completed in the 18 months before the end of hostilities.
● The type was produced in two principal variants, the Ki-84-I (four sub-variants, each with increasingly powerful armament) and the Ki-84-II, which had a wooden rear fuselage and fittings in an effort to reduce the drain on Japan's dwindling reserves of strategic light alloys.
● The last version was the Ki-116, a converted Ki-84-Ia with a lighter engine.

SPECIFICATIONS

TYPE: *Single-seat interceptor fighter/fighter-bomber*

POWERPLANT: *One 1416 kW (1,900 hp) Nakajima Ha-45-23 18-cylinder radial piston engine*

PERFORMANCE: *Maximum speed: 631 km/h (391 mph) at 6120 m (20,000 ft); Range: 2168 km (1,350 miles); Service ceiling: 10,500 m (34,500 ft)*

WEIGHTS: *Empty: 2660 kg (5,830 lb); Loaded: 3890 kg (8,558 lb)*

ARMAMENT: *Two 12.7 mm (.50 cal.) Ho-103 synchronized nose machine guns and two wing-mounted 20 mm (0.79 in) Ho-5 cannon (later models had four cannon), plus underwing racks for two 250 kg (551 lb) bombs or two 190 litre (50 gallon) drop-tanks*

DIMENSIONS: *Span: 11.24 m (36 ft 10 in); Length: 9.92 m (32 ft 6 in); Height: 3.39 m (11 ft 1 in); Wing area: 21.00 m² (226 sq ft)*

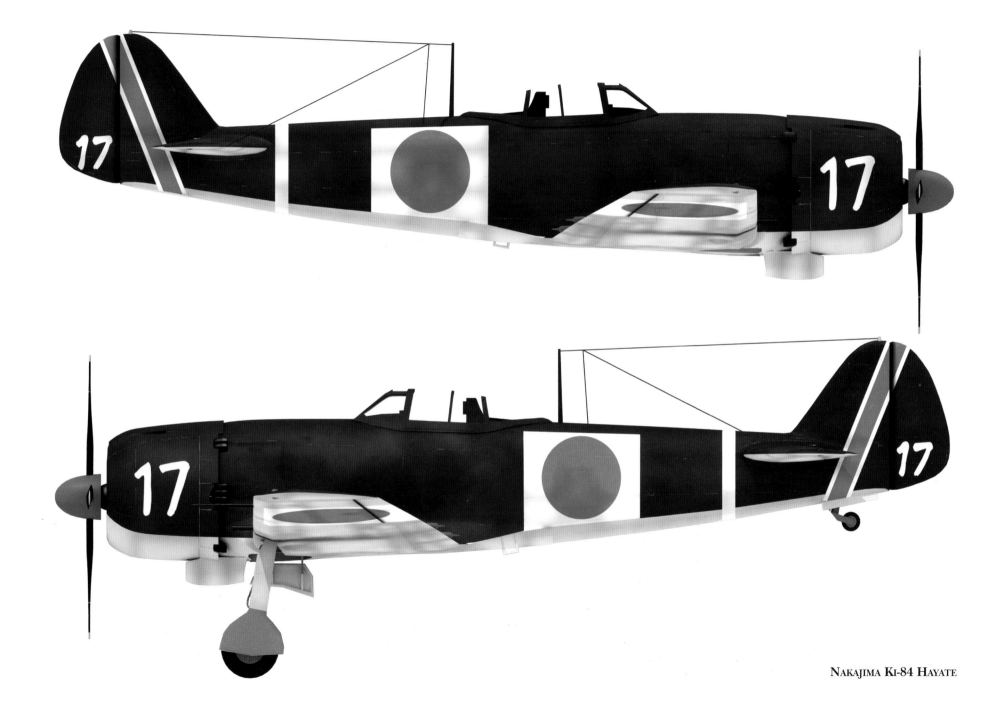

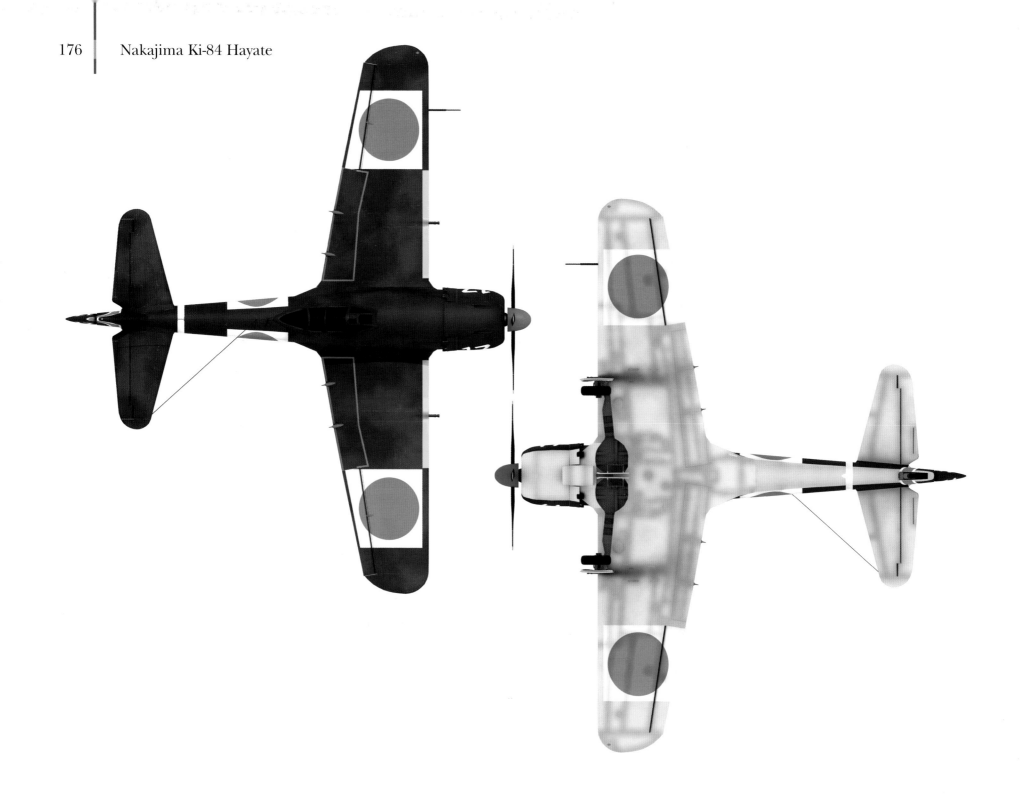

Relentless Defence

This Hayate was assigned to the air defence of the Japanese home islands in 1945, and belonged to the 520th Special Air Defence Fighter Squadron. Its pilots had orders to ram American B-29 bombers after the fighters had expended their ammunition.

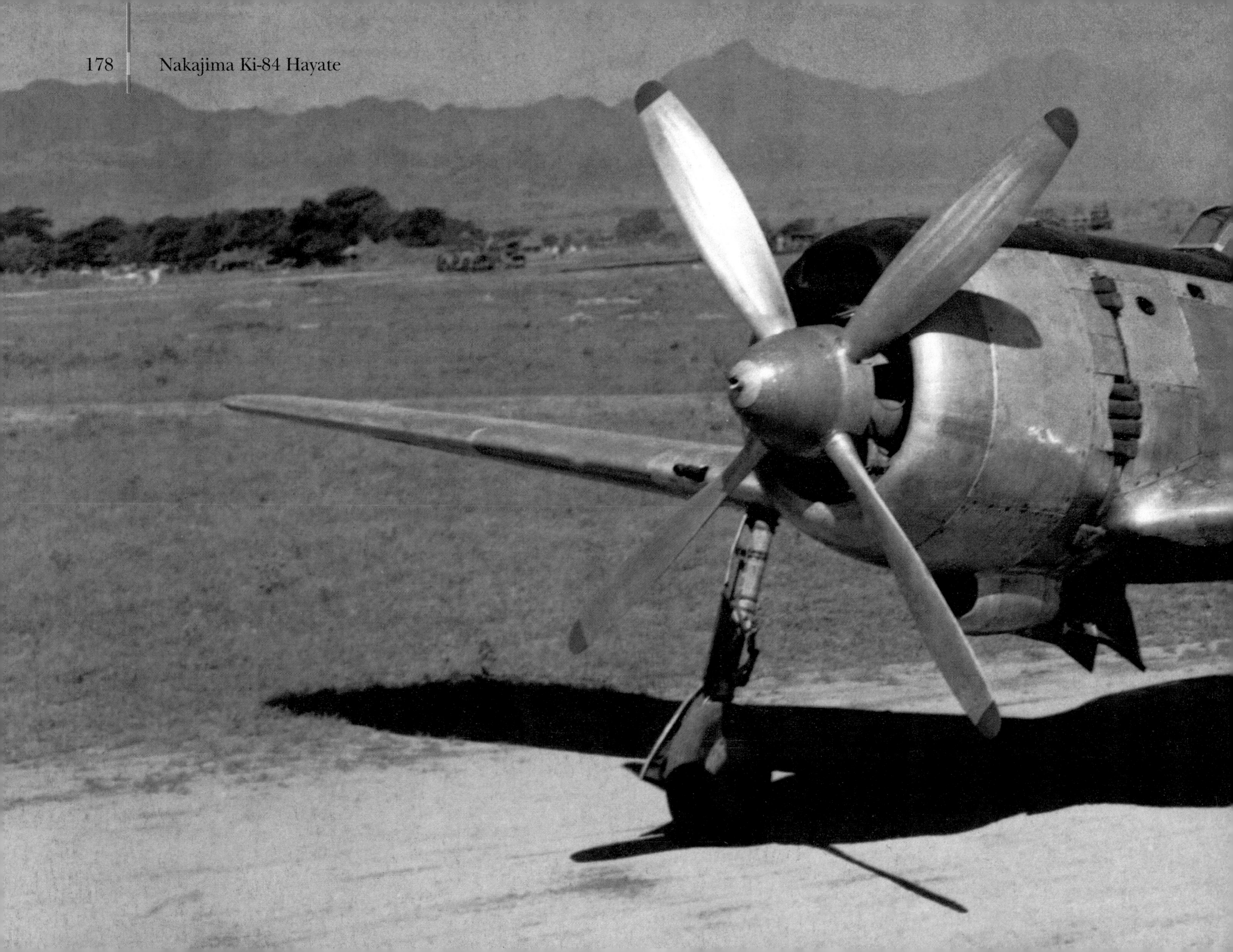

UNREALIZED POTENTIAL

The US Technical Air Intelligence Command evaluated the Nakajima Ki-84 Hayate following the end of World War II, and American test pilots were full of admiration for the aircraft. With its large four-bladed propeller and powerful engine, the Hayate was very much in the same league as the American fighters it had to face, but it had lost none of the startling manoeuvrability of earlier Japanese fighter types – in particular, the Mitsubishi Zero. It was never used to its fullest advantage for a variety of reasons, not least of which was that by the time the Hayate entered service the best Japanese army pilots were dead, and their replacements were poorly trained and unable to get the best out of what was a truly splendid aircraft.

North American P-51 Mustang

Produced in response to a 1940 RAF requirement for a fast, heavily armed fighter able to operate effectively at altitudes in excess of 6100 m (20,000 ft), the North American P-51 Mustang became one of the most famous fighters of World War II. The first two USAAF Mustang variants, both optimized for ground attack and designated A-36A and P-51A, were fitted with Allison engines. Trials with Mustangs fitted with Packard-built Rolls-Royce Merlin 61 engines showed a dramatic improvement in performance, and production of the Merlin-powered P-51B got under way in the autumn of 1942. In December 1943, P-51Bs of the 354th Fighter Group flew their first operational escort mission from England, escorting B-17s to Kiel and back.

- The major production model, the P-51D, began to arrive in England in the late spring of 1944 and quickly became the standard equipment of the USAAF Eighth Fighter Command.
- Mustangs operating from the captured Japanese islands of Iwo Jima and Okinawa used similar tactics from April 1945, escorting B-29s to their targets and neutralizing the Japanese air force on the ground.
- The Mustang continued to serve with some 20 air forces around the world for years after the end of World War II, and gave valiant service during the early months of the Korean War with US, Australian, South African and South Korean air units.

SPECIFICATIONS

Type: *Single-seat long-range escort fighter and fighter-bomber*

Powerplant: *One 1186 kW (1,590 hp) Packard V-1650-7 (US-built Rolls-Royce Merlin 61) inverted-vee 12-cylinder inline water-cooled piston engine*

Performance: *Maximum speed: 716 km/h (445 mph) at 7620 m (25,000 ft); Combat radius: 525 km (326 miles) on internal fuel or 1210 km (752 miles) with two 491 litre (108 gallon) tanks; Service ceiling: 12,770 m (41,900 ft)*

Weights: *Empty: 3232 kg (7,125 lb); Loaded: 5265 kg (11,607 lb)*

Armament: *Six 12.7 mm (.50 cal.) Browning M2 machine guns in wings; two 227 kg (500 lb) bombs or eight 75 mm (2.95 in) rockets*

Dimensions: *Span: 11.29 m (37 ft); Length: 9.83 m (32 ft 3 in); Height: 3.71 m (12 ft 2 in); Wing area: 21.83 m² (235 sq ft)*

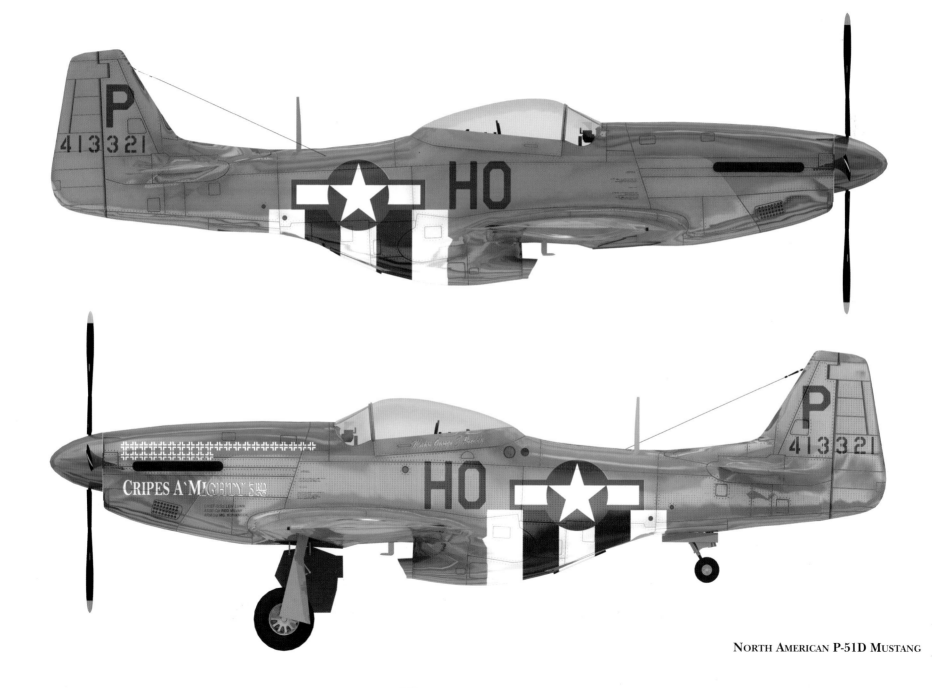

NORTH AMERICAN P-51D MUSTANG

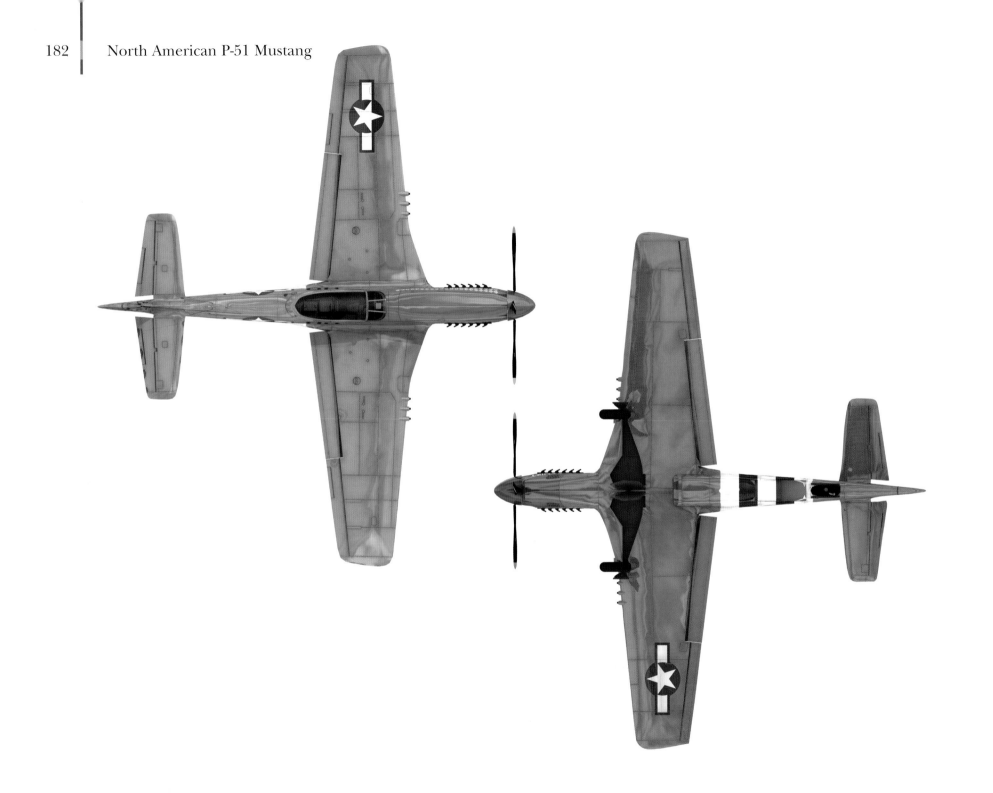

A Sterling Escort

The 352nd Fighter Group was armed with the P-51 Mustang from spring of 1944. Seen here is a P-51D of the group's 487th Fighter Squadron, which operated its Mustangs from Bodney, Norfolk, until moving to Belgium in January 1945.

413410

2 • C

DAYLIGHT VICTOR

There is no doubt at all that the Merlin-engined P-51D Mustang won the daylight battle over Germany. Operating from bases in England and Italy, it not only provided fighter escort for the bombers engaged in a two-pronged assault on Hitler's Reich, but also hunted the Luftwaffe on its own airfields. On 6 March 1944, Mustangs appeared for the first time over Berlin and took part in one of the most bitterly contested air battles of the war, with 200 German fighters taking on 660 heavy bombers and their escort. When the battle ended, the Americans had lost 69 bombers and 11 fighters, but the Germans lost 80 aircraft – almost half of their defensive force.

Northrop P-61 Black Widow

The Northrop P-61 Black Widow was designed from the outset as a night fighter. The P-61 served in all theatres of war, but scored spectacular successes in the Pacific. A lack of Allied night fighters had made it relatively safe for Japanese bombers to operate under cover of darkness, until the P-61 took on its role as a night intruder, attacking enemy shipping as well as targets on land. On 29 November 1944, Black Widows were ordered to make a night attack on a Japanese convoy in Leyte Gulf. The convoy, consisting of two escort destroyers and a number of smaller vessels, was heading towards Ormoc to land reinforcement troops and supplies. The convoy was duly harassed throughout the night, preventing landing of its troops.

- The radar operator had the best position in the P-61, installed above and behind the pilot with an excellent forward view. His SCR-720 radar was an advanced piece of equipment, having anti-jamming features which would seek out an enemy aircraft even if the latter were using countermeasures.
- The P-61 had a massive spread of wing. It helped to give the fighter its deadly appearance, fostering the impression that here was a fighting machine designed solely for war.
- In the United Kingdom, P-61s were used in action against V-1 flying bombs in the late summer of 1944 before deploying to the Continent, as the night-fighter component of the US Ninth Army Air Force.

SPECIFICATIONS

TYPE: *Three-seat night-fighter*

POWERPLANT: *Two 1491 kW (2,000 hp) Pratt & Whitney R-2800-65 Double Wasp 18-cylinder radial engines*

PERFORMANCE: *Maximum speed: 589 km/h (365 mph) at 6096 m (20,000 ft); Range: 1513 km (940 miles) (2172 km/1,350 miles with drop-tanks); Service ceiling: 12,445 m (40,800 ft)*

WEIGHTS: *Empty: 9654 kg (21,239 lb); Loaded: 13,471 kg (29,636 lb); Maximum take-off: 16,420 kg (36,124 lb)*

ARMAMENT: *four 20 mm (0.79 in) M2 cannon each with 200 rounds; dorsal barbette with four 12.7 mm (.50 cal.) machine guns each with 560 rounds; pylons for 454 kg (1,000 lb) of bombs, rockets or other weapons*

DIMENSIONS: *Span: 20.11 m (66 ft); Length: 15.11 m (50 ft); Height: 4.47 m (15 ft); Wing area: 61.53 m² (662 sq ft)*

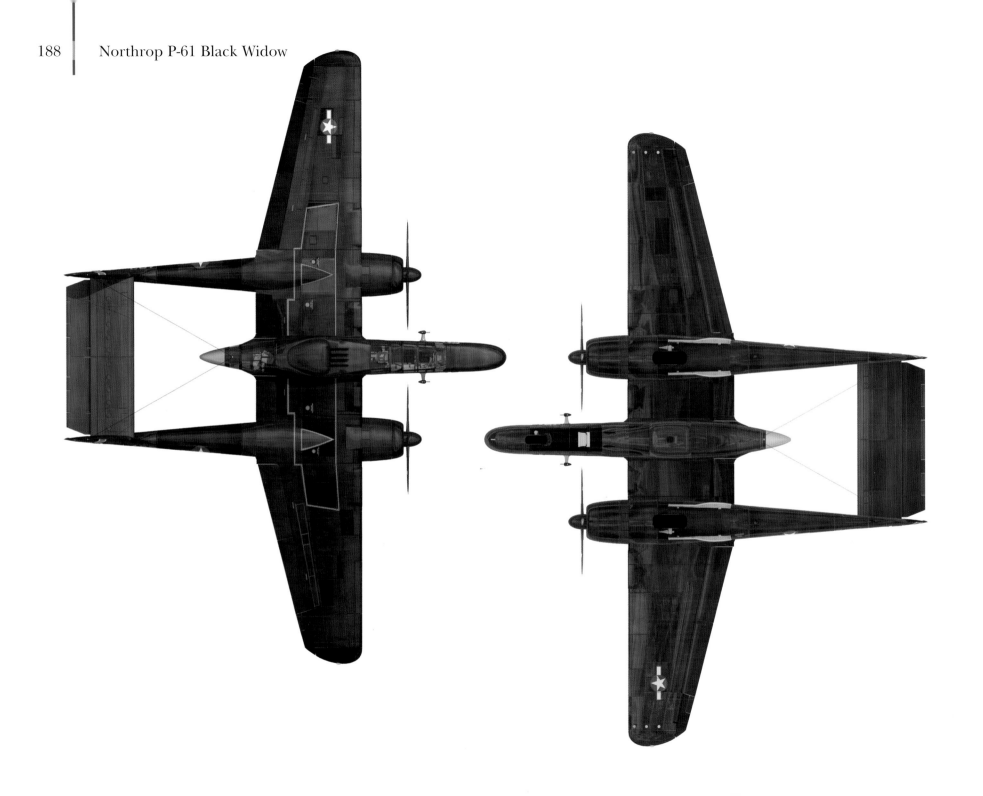

Dogged Determination
A P-61 of the 418th Night Fighter Squadron. This unit operated in New Guinea and the Philippines during the Pacific war, and was probably the hardest-worked of all the Black Widow squadrons, seeing considerable action against enemy intruders.

239728

NIGHT CAMOUFLAGE

Attempts were made to give the Northrop P-61 a 'stealthy' appearance through the use of special camouflage. Night fighter camouflage was a subject for much debate during the early years of World War II, and the Office of Scientific Research's Camouflage Section at the Massachusetts Institute of Technology was given the task of developing a paint that would render a night fighter 'invisible' when caught in searchlight beams. The best finish was found to be a very glossy black, but before this was recommended the first Black Widows were painted in olive drab and neutral grey.

Republic P-47 Thunderbolt

One of the truly great fighter aircraft of World War II, the Republic P-47 Thunderbolt represented the culmination of a line of aircraft that had its origins in two 1936 designs, the Seversky P-35 and P-43. Examples of the initial production version, the P-47B, were issued to the USAAF 56th Fighter Group in June 1942, and in December 1942–January 1943 it deployed to England, flying its first combat mission on 13 April 1943. The arrival of the P-47, fitted with a long-range belly tank, in the United Kingdom greatly increased the survival chances of US daylight bombers penetrating into hostile air space. P-47s also operated in the Pacific theatre from 1943 until the end of the war. The major production version was the P-47D, which was also used by the RAF in Burma as the Thunderbolt I and II.

- Overall P-47 production, which ended in December 1945, was 15,660 aircraft. About two-thirds of these, almost all P-47Ds, survived the war and found their way into the air forces of Brazil, Chile, Colombia, Dominica, Ecuador, Mexico, Peru, Turkey and Yugoslavia.
- France also used the P-47D in its operations against dissidents in Algeria during the 1950s.
- During World War II, the Soviet Union received 195 P-47s out of 203 allocated; some were lost en route.

SPECIFICATIONS

TYPE: *Single-seat fighter and fighter-bomber*

POWERPLANT: *One 1715 kW (2,535 hp) Pratt & Whitney R-2800-59 Double Wasp 18-cylinder radial engine*

PERFORMANCE: *Maximum speed: 697 km/h (430 mph); Range: 3000 km (1,860 miles) with drop-tanks; Service ceiling: 12,800 m (42,000 ft)*

WEIGHTS: *Empty: 4853 kg (10,660 lb); Loaded: 7938 kg (17,500 lb)*

ARMAMENT: *Eight 12.7 mm (.50 cal.) Browning M2 machine guns with 267 to 500 rounds; plus provision for maximum external load of 1134 kg (2,500 lb) including bombs, napalm or eight rockets*

DIMENSIONS: *Span: 12.42 m (40 ft 9 in); Length: 11.02 m (36 ft 2 in); Height: 4.30 m (14 ft 2 in); Wing area: 27.87 m² (300 sq ft)*

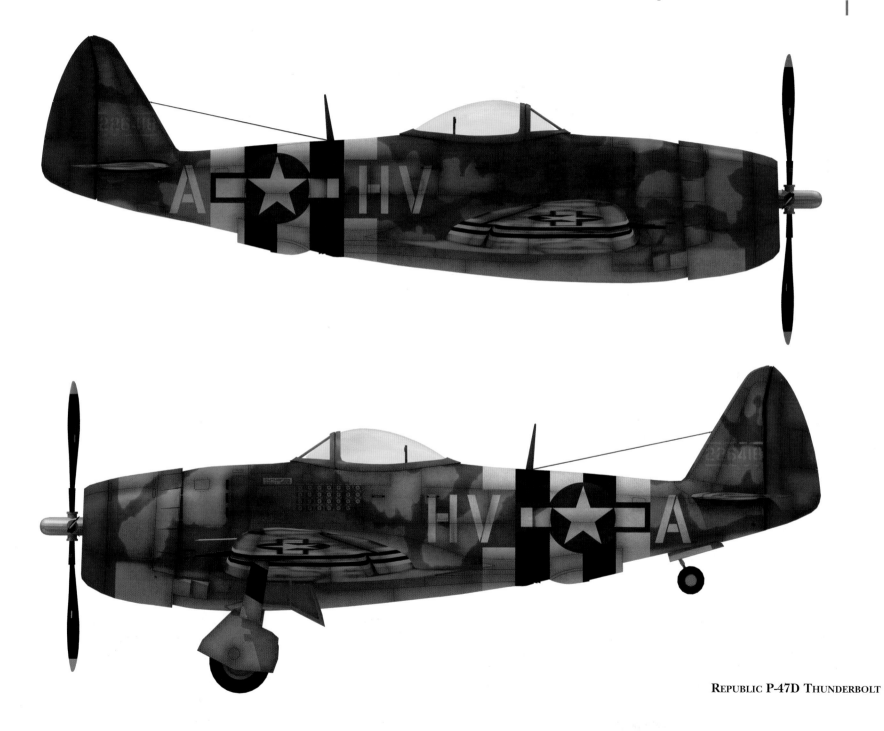

REPUBLIC P-47D THUNDERBOLT

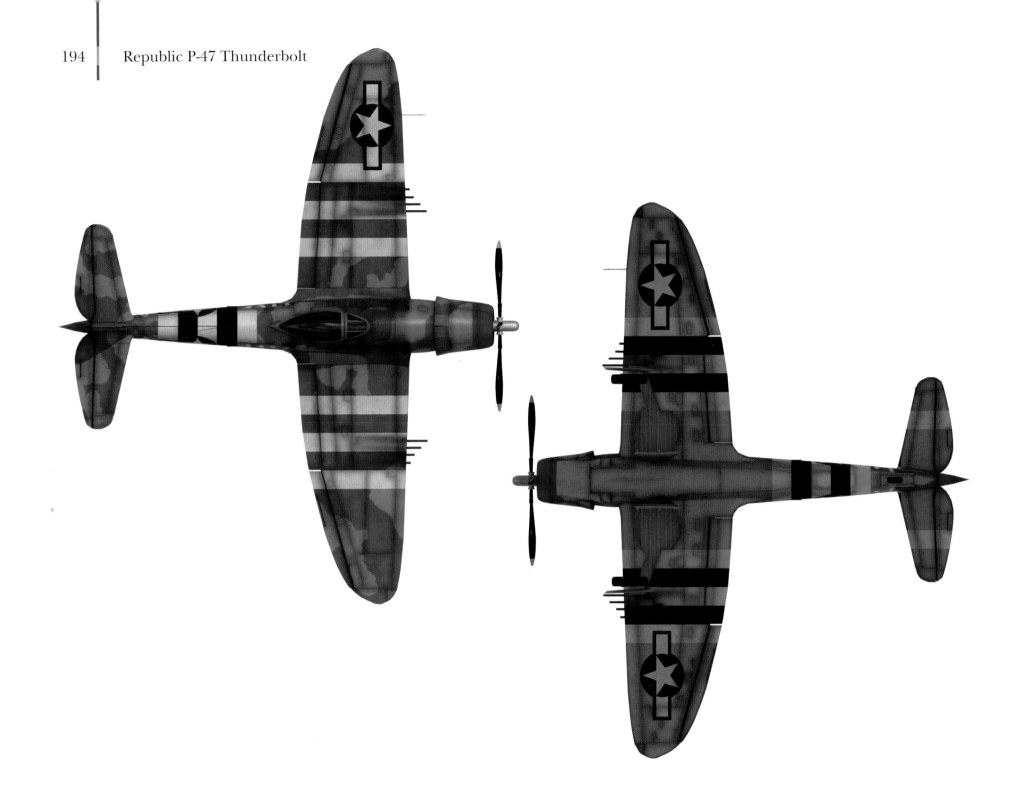

Deployment to the United Kingdom
A P-47D Thunderbolt of the 56th Fighter Group, Boxted, Essex. The code letters 'HV' were carried by the Group's 61st Fighter Squadron between February 1943 and September 1945.

488576

PRODIGIOUS WORK RATE

From their first operational sortie over Europe until the end of the fighting in the Pacific in August 1945, Thunderbolts flew 546,000 combat sorties, dropped 132,000 tons of bombs, launched 60,000 rockets and expended more than 135 million rounds of ammunition. In the European theatre alone, from D-Day (6 June 1944) to VE Day (8 May 1945), the Thunderbolt was credited with destroying 9000 locomotives, 86,000 railway wagons, and 6,000 armoured vehicles. In all theatres of war, it pilots claimed destruction of 3752 enemy aircraft in the air and a further 3315 on the ground. During its two years of operations over Europe, the 56th FG destroyed more enemy aircraft than any other fighter group of the Eighth USAAF. The 56th's motto, 'Cave Tonitrum' (Beware the Thunderbolt) was well justified.

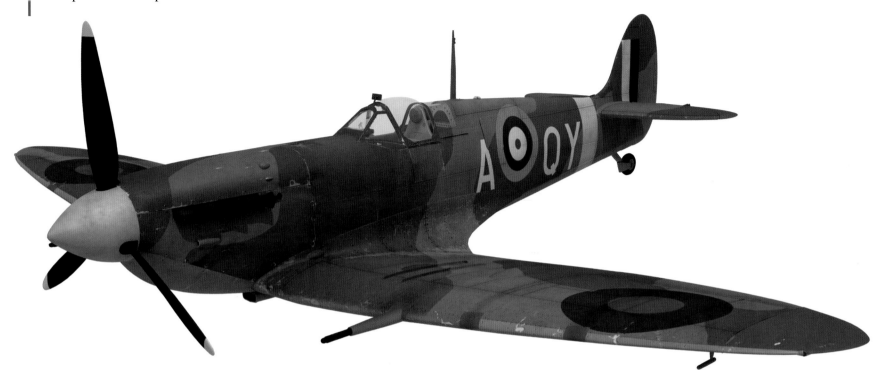

Supermarine Spitfire

Arguably the most charismatic fighter aircraft of all time, the Spitfire will for ever be synonymous with the Royal Air Force's victory in the Battle of Britain, in which it fought alongside the less glamorous Hawker Hurricane. During the battle, from 1 July to 31 October 1940, 361 of the 747 Spitfires delivered to Fighter Command were destroyed, not all in combat. The Mk I Spitfire bore the brunt of the fighting; the Mk II, with a more powerful version of the Rolls-Royce engine, was issued to the squadrons of Fighter Command in September 1940. The major production version was the Mk V, which began to reach the squadrons in March 1941 and was converted from Mk I and II airframes. But it failed to provide the overall superiority Fighter Command needed so badly. The solution was to marry a Mk V airframe with a Merlin 61 engine. The result was the Spitfire Mk IX, which for a stopgap aircraft turned out to be a resounding success.

- At high altitude, where many combats took place, the Spitfire Mk V was inferior to the Bf 109F on most counts, and several squadrons equipped with it took a severe mauling during the summer of 1941.
- From the Mk XII onwards, the Spitfire was powered by the Rolls-Royce Griffon engine.
- The last variants of the Spitfire, produced until 1947, were the Mks 21, 22 and 24. They bore hardly any resemblance to the prototype Mk I of a decade earlier.

SPECIFICATIONS

TYPE: *Single-seat fighter/interceptor*

POWERPLANT: *one 1103 kW (1,440 hp) Rolls-Royce Merlin 45 Vee piston engine*

PERFORMANCE: *594 km/h (374 mph) at 5945 m (13,000 ft); 1827 km (1,135 miles); Service ceiling: 11,125 m (37,000 ft)*

WEIGHTS: *Empty 2267 kg (5,000 lb); loaded 2911 kg (6,400 lb)*

ARMAMENT: *Four 7.7-mm (.303 cal) Browning machine-guns and two 20 mm (0.78 in) cannon*

DIMENSIONS: *Span: 11.23 m (36 ft 10 in) ; Length: 9.12 m (29 ft 11 in); Height: 3.02 m (11 ft 5 in) ; Wing area: 22.48 m² (242 sq ft)*

SUPERMARINE SPITFIRE MK VB

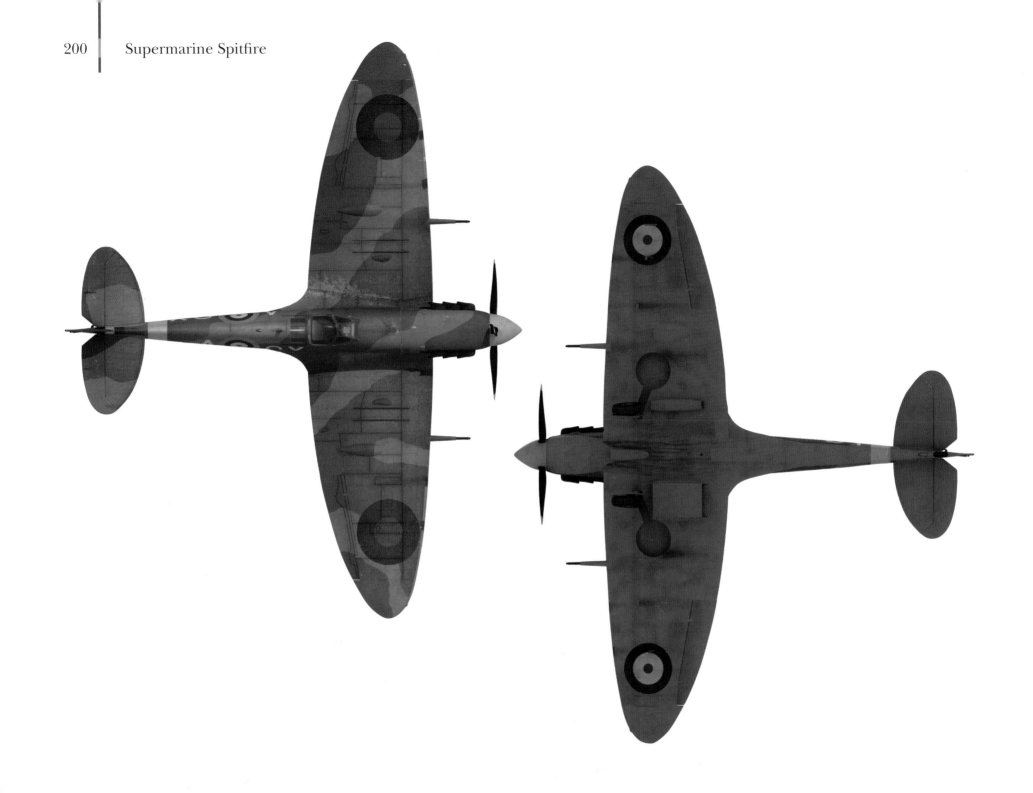

Spitfire Squadron
The Royal Air Force's No. 616 Squadron, later to become the world's first operational jet fighter squadron with Gloster Meteors, flew Spitfires from October 1939 until the summer of 1944. Seen here is a Mk VB.

ELLIPTICAL WINGS

This image of a Spitfire Mk XIV in flight emphasises the clean and elegant lines of this iconic fighter aircraft.

A key feature of the Supermarine Spitfire was its excellent manoeuvrability. Its wing was elliptical, a shape that the Spitfire's designer, Reginald Mitchell, had selected once before, in a 1929 project for a six-engine flying boat. It is not clear why Mitchell chose the elliptical shape, as it was difficult to engineer and calculations showed that it offered an aerodynamic performance at high speed less than one per cent better than a wing with a straight taper; however, there is no doubt that it was successful. In the original design, the wing was perfectly elliptical – in other words, formed from two half ellipses with a swept main spar – but was redesigned to produce the familiar Spitfire wing shape, the main spar being straight along the main axis.

Vought F4U Corsair

Although tricky to handle as a carrier-based fighter-bomber, the F4U Corsair proved to be one of the superlative combat aircraft of the Pacific war, particularly in the hands of the US Marine Corps. Carrier trials began in September 1942; the first Corsair unit, Marine Fighting Squadron VMF-214, was declared combat-ready in December, deploying to Guadalcanal in February 1943. After trials with VF-12, the Corsair became operational with Navy Fighting Squadron VF-17 in April 1943, deploying to a land base in New Georgia in September. Of the 12,681 Corsairs built during World War II, 2012 were supplied to the Royal Navy, equipping 19 squadrons of the Fleet Air Arm; some of these aircraft were diverted to equip three squadrons of the Royal New Zealand Air Force, operating in the Solomons. RN Corsair squadrons provided cover for Fleet Air Arm attacks on the German battleship *Tirpitz* in 1944, and subsequently deployed to the Pacific with a British carrier task force in 1945, taking part in the final offensives against Japan.

- Variants of the Corsair included the F4U-1C cannon-armed fighter, F4U-1D fighter-bomber, F4U-2 night fighter, F4U-3 high-altitude research version, and F4U-4 fighter.
- Post-war variants of the Corsair gave tremendous service during the Korean War of 1950–53.
- Corsairs supplied to the French navy saw combat during the Anglo-French Suez operation of 1956.

SPECIFICATIONS

TYPE: *Single-seat, carrier-operable fighter-bomber*

POWERPLANT: *One 1492 kW (2,000 hp) Pratt & Whitney R-2800-8 Double Wasp 18-cylinder radial piston engine*

PERFORMANCE: *Maximum speed: 671 km/h (417 mph) at 6605 m (20,000 ft); Range: 1650 km (1,010 miles); Service ceiling: 11,247 m (37,000 ft)*

WEIGHTS: *Empty: 4074 kg (9,000 lb); Loaded: 6350 kg (14,000 lb)*

ARMAMENT: *Six 12.7 mm (.50 cal.) Browning M2 machine guns with 400 rounds (outboard) and 375 rounds (inboard) per gun; up to 1800 kg (4,000 lb) of bombs or rockets*

DIMENSIONS: *Span: 12.49 m (41 ft); Length: 10.16 m (33 ft 5 in); Height: 4.90 m (15 ft 1 in); Wing area: 29.17 m² (314 sq ft)*

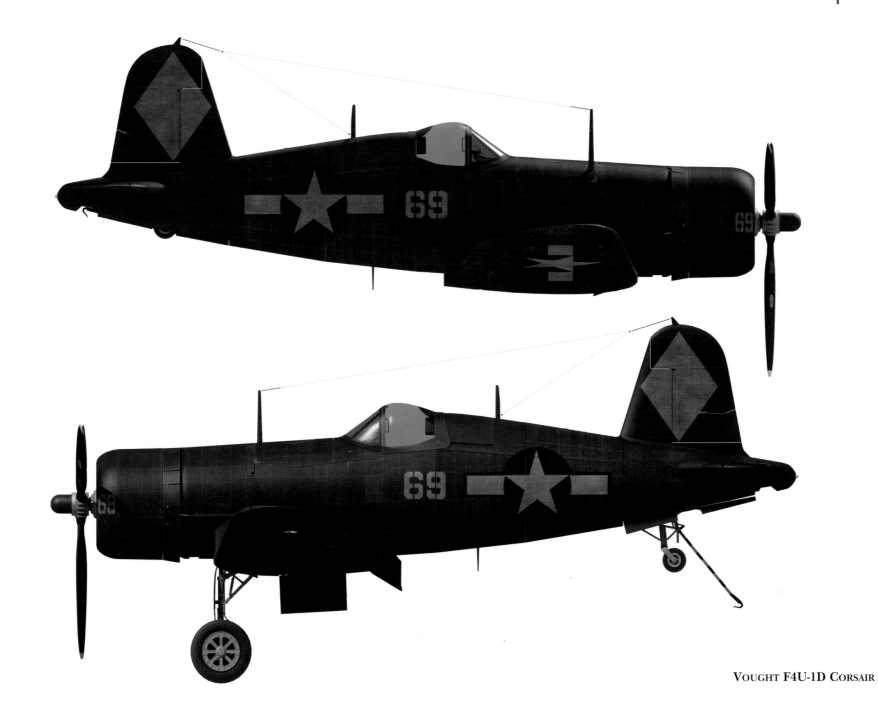

VOUGHT F4U-1D CORSAIR

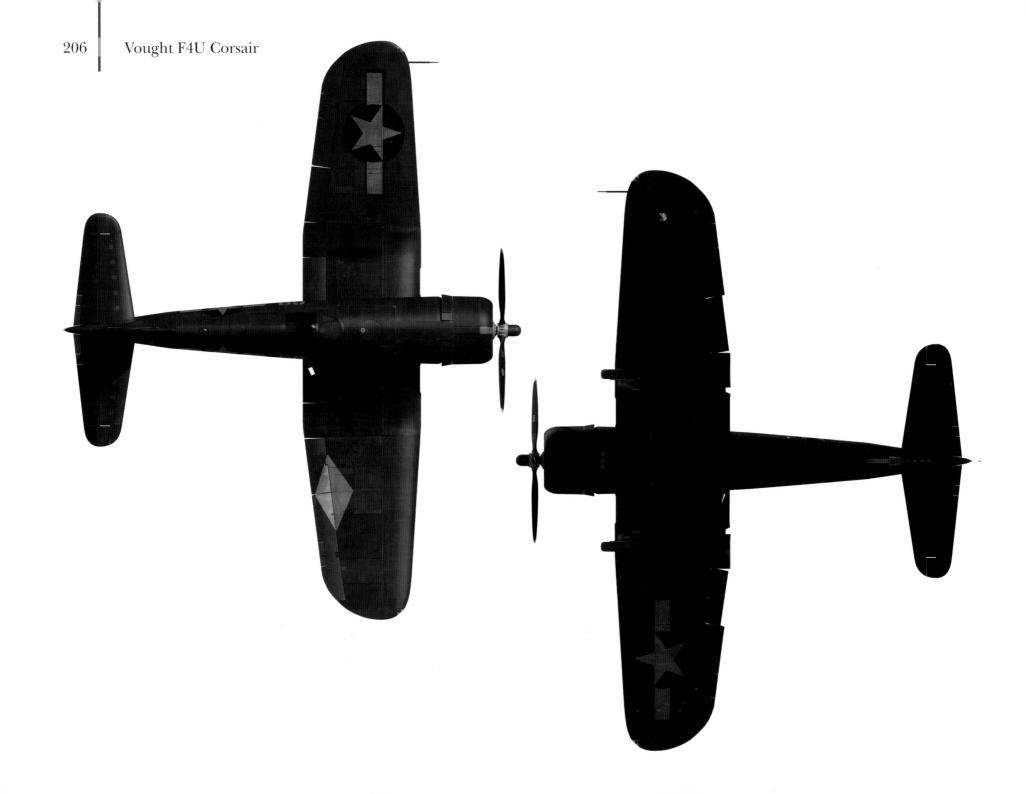

Providing Support from Land
An F-4U-1D Corsair of US Marine Fighter Squadron VMF-214, the first combat unit to equip with the type. Marine Corsair squadrons mostly operated from land bases in support of ground forces.

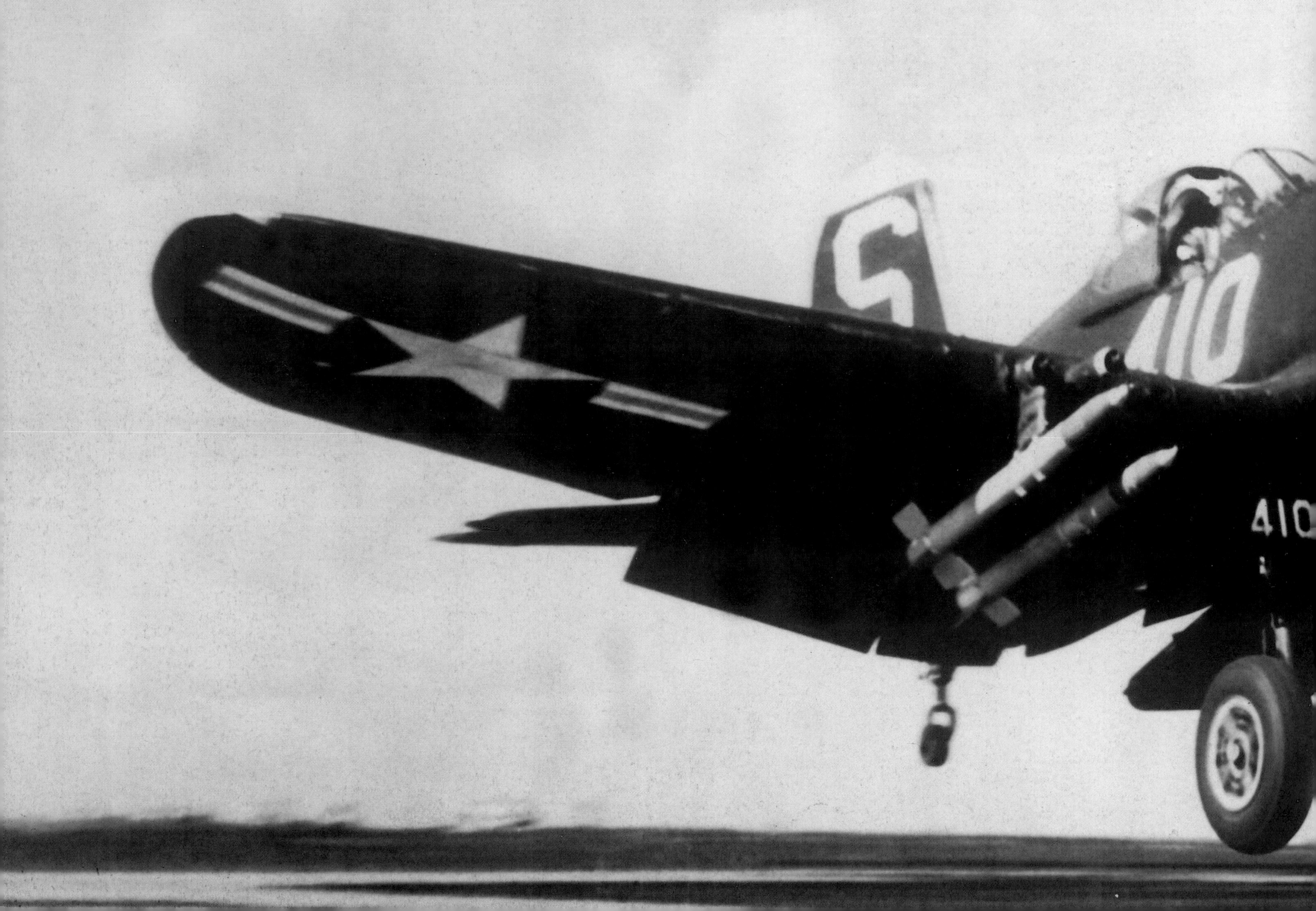
410

CAREFUL HANDLING

Early-model Vought F4U Corsairs had limited visibility, with the engine blocking the view over the nose. In later models, the pilot sat in a higher position under a bulged clear-view canopy, and the engine was drooped by 2.5 degrees to improve the pilot's forward vision. The Corsair had a nasty stall characteristic of rapidly dropping its port wing, and the pilot needed to be aware of this as the big fighter slowed down to carrier landing speeds. If the pilot advanced the throttle suddenly, the torque from the engine and propeller could actually cause the aircraft to flip upside down. The arrester hook, fitted for carrier operations, was removed when the Marine Corps began operating the fighter from land bases. The solid rubber tailwheel was replaced by a pneumatic one because the solid version tended to tear up easily on rough surfaces.

Westland Lysander

The Westland Lysander was the Royal Air Force's standard army co-operation type at World War II's outbreak. Four squadrons deployed to France in 1939 in support of the Air Component of the British Expeditionary Force, followed by a fifth early in 1940. They suffered severe losses during the German offensive of May 1940; of the 170 aircraft sent to the Continent, only 50 returned to England. Many losses were sustained when the Lysanders were tasked with dropping light bombs on the advancing enemy columns, where they fell easy prey to the German flak and patrolling fighters. On the night of 19/20 October 1940, a Lysander was used for the first time to pick up an agent, Philip Schneidau, from a field near Montigny, France. The aircraft continued in this role until the war's end, operating in the Far East as well as Europe.

- By early 1942, all special-duties Lysanders were concentrated in a single squadron, No. 161. They flew from Tangmere, England, on their cross-Channel missions to deliver and collect secret agents.
- Special-duties Lysanders of No. 148 Squadron operated in Greece in 1944, while in the Far East Lysanders were used by No. 357 Squadron for pickup operations in Burma.
- In June 1945, one Lysander mission involved evacuating wounded Japanese nurses from a Burmese airstrip inside enemy-held territory.

SPECIFICATIONS

TYPE: *Army co-operation aircraft*

POWERPLANT: *One 649 kW (870 hp) Bristol Mercury XX radial piston engine*

PERFORMANCE: *Maximum speed: 341 km/h (211 mph) at 1525 m (5,000 ft); Range: 966 km (600 miles); Service ceiling: 6655 m (21,800 ft)*

WEIGHTS: *Empty: 1980 kg (4,356 lb); maximum take-off: 2866 kg (6,305 lb)*

ARMAMENT: *Four 7.7 mm (.303 cal.) Browning machine guns (one in each wheel spat and two on trainable mount in rear cockpit); up to 227 kg (500 lb) of flares, rocket projectiles or bombs*

DIMENSIONS: *Span: 15.24 m (50 ft); Length: 9.30 m (30 ft 6 in); Height: 4.42 m (14 ft 6 in); Wing area: 24.15 m² (260 sq ft)*

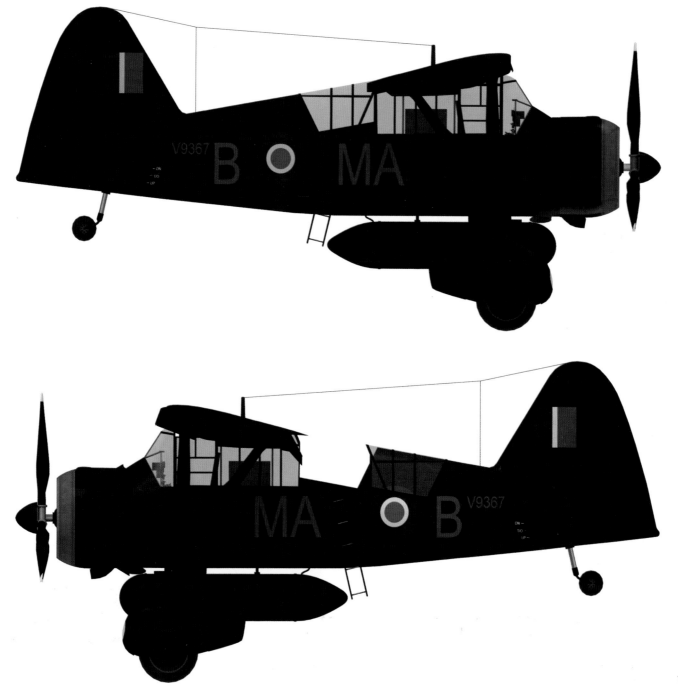

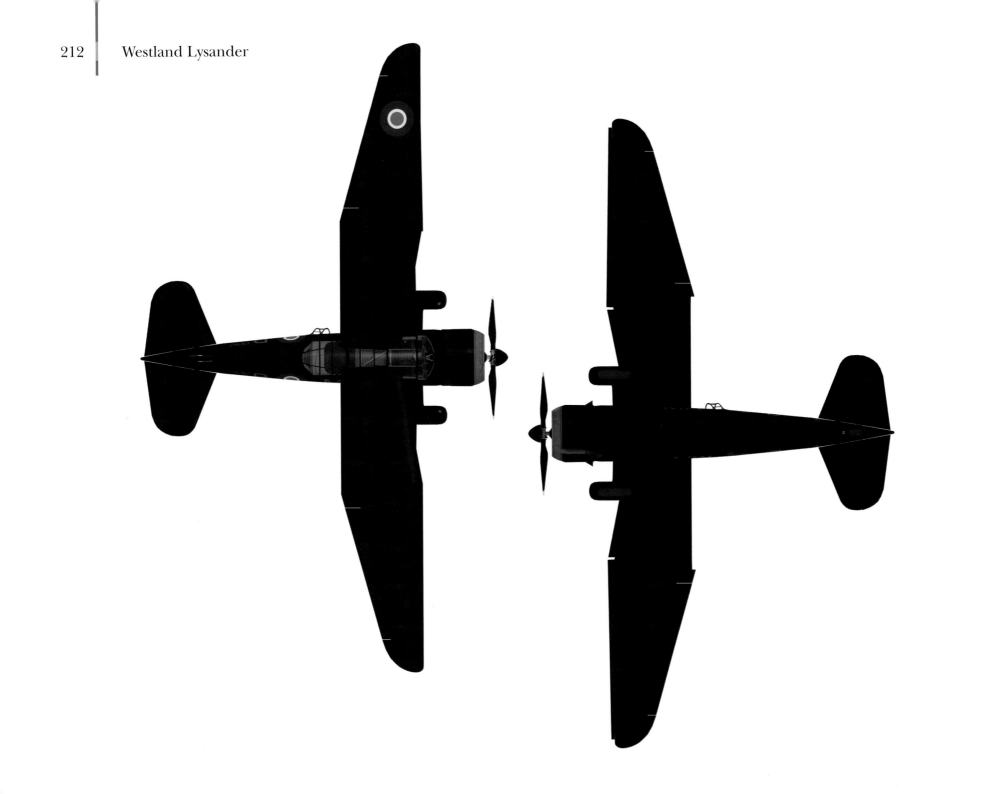

Special Access for Special Duties

A Westland Lysander of No. 161 (SD) Squadron. Special-duties Lysanders had a metal ladder fixed to the port side of the fuselage to facilitate access to the rear cockpit when a pickup was being made.

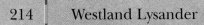

PERFECT FOR PICKUPS

The Westland Lysander was ideally suited to pickup operations. Its wooden, fabric-covered wings had full-span automatic leading-edge slats that operated from any position between closed and fully open, allowing maximum use of this lift device, while the flaps could be lowered to any position between fully up and fully down, depending on speed. The Lysander was therefore able to land and take off at extremely low speeds, operating comfortably from pastures, fields and even forest clearings. The view from the high-set cockpit was also excellent, and the in-board wing leading edges were tapered so that the pilot could see through the top of the canopy during very steep turns, another advantage when a sharp getaway was needed.

Yakovlev Yak-3

The Russians were late in developing effective monoplane fighters in the same class as Britain's Hurricane and Spitfire, and Germany's Bf 109, but Aleksandr Yakovlev's attractive designs soon redressed the situation. The first was the Yak-1 Krasavyets (Beauty), which made its first public appearance during an air display on 7 November 1940. It was Yakovlev's first fighter design, and it earned him the Order of Lenin, the gift of a Zis car and a prize of 100,000 roubles. The first Yak-3s reached the front line during early summer 1943, in time to take part in the Battle of Kursk. It was not until the spring of 1944 that the fighter was available in substantial numbers, but it quickly proved itself in combat.

- The Yak-3 rarely operated above 3500 m (11,500 ft). Below this it was markedly more manoeuvrable than either the FW 190A or Bf 109G; in fact, it was probably the most manoeuvrable fighter of World War II.
- As well as performing the role of interceptor, the Yak-3 was extensively employed in close support of the ground forces, and for the escort of Pe-2 and Il-2 assault aircraft, one formation of Yak-3s preceding the bombers and attacking German fighter airfields, while another provided closer escort.
- The Yak-3 airframe, married to a captured German Junkers Jumo 004 turbojet, became the first Soviet jet fighter.

SPECIFICATIONS

TYPE: *Single-seat fighter and fighter-bomber*

POWERPLANT: *One 969 kW (1,300 hp) Klimov VK-105PF-2 V-12 piston engine*

PERFORMANCE: *Maximum speed: 655 km/h (407 mph); Range: 900 km (559 miles); Service ceiling: 10,700 m (35,105 ft)*

WEIGHTS: *Empty: 2105 kg (4,641 lb); Maximum take-off: 2670 kg (5,864 lb)*

ARMAMENT: *One 20 mm (0.79 in) ShVAK cannon; two ShKAS 12.7 mm (.50 cal.) machine guns*

DIMENSIONS: *Span: 9.19 m (30 ft 2 in); Length: 8.48 m (27 ft 9 in); Height: 2.41m (7 ft 11 in); Wing area: 14.85 m² (159.84 sq ft)*

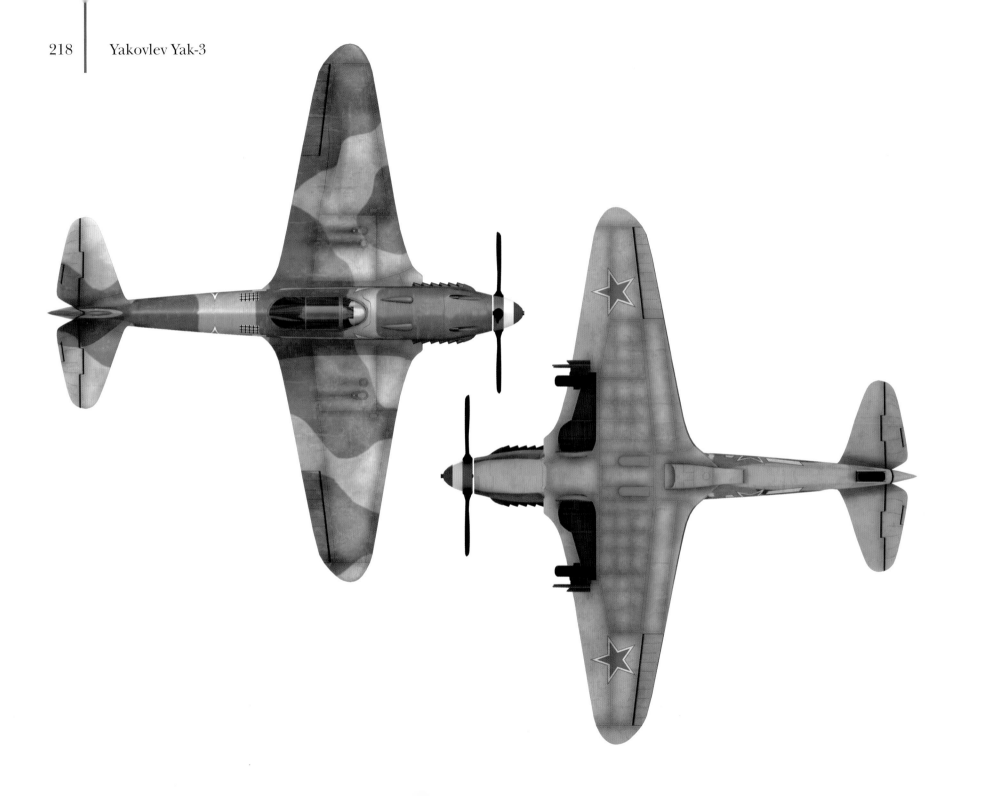

In French Hands

This Yakovlev Yak-3 was flown by Groupe de Chasse GC3 'Normandie-Niemen', the French fighter unit that fought with distinction on the Russian front in World War II. Between April 1943, when it first went into action, and the end of the war in May 1945, the unit destroyed 273 enemy aircraft.

FIGHTING ATTRIBUTES

The Yak-3 went into combat for the first time towards the end of Operation Citadel, the German offensive at Kursk in June 1943. Its pilots were enthusiastic about its fighting qualities. Ideally suited to low-altitude combat, its light stick pressure produced fast and accurate snap rolls, and all combat manoeuvres could be executed precisely and smoothly; however, the Yak-3 demanded careful handling at low speed. Its stalling speed was high, and it tended to drop a wing on the approach unless airspeed was kept up. It also had a tendency to swing on takeoff and landing, and ground loops were not uncommon among experienced pilots.

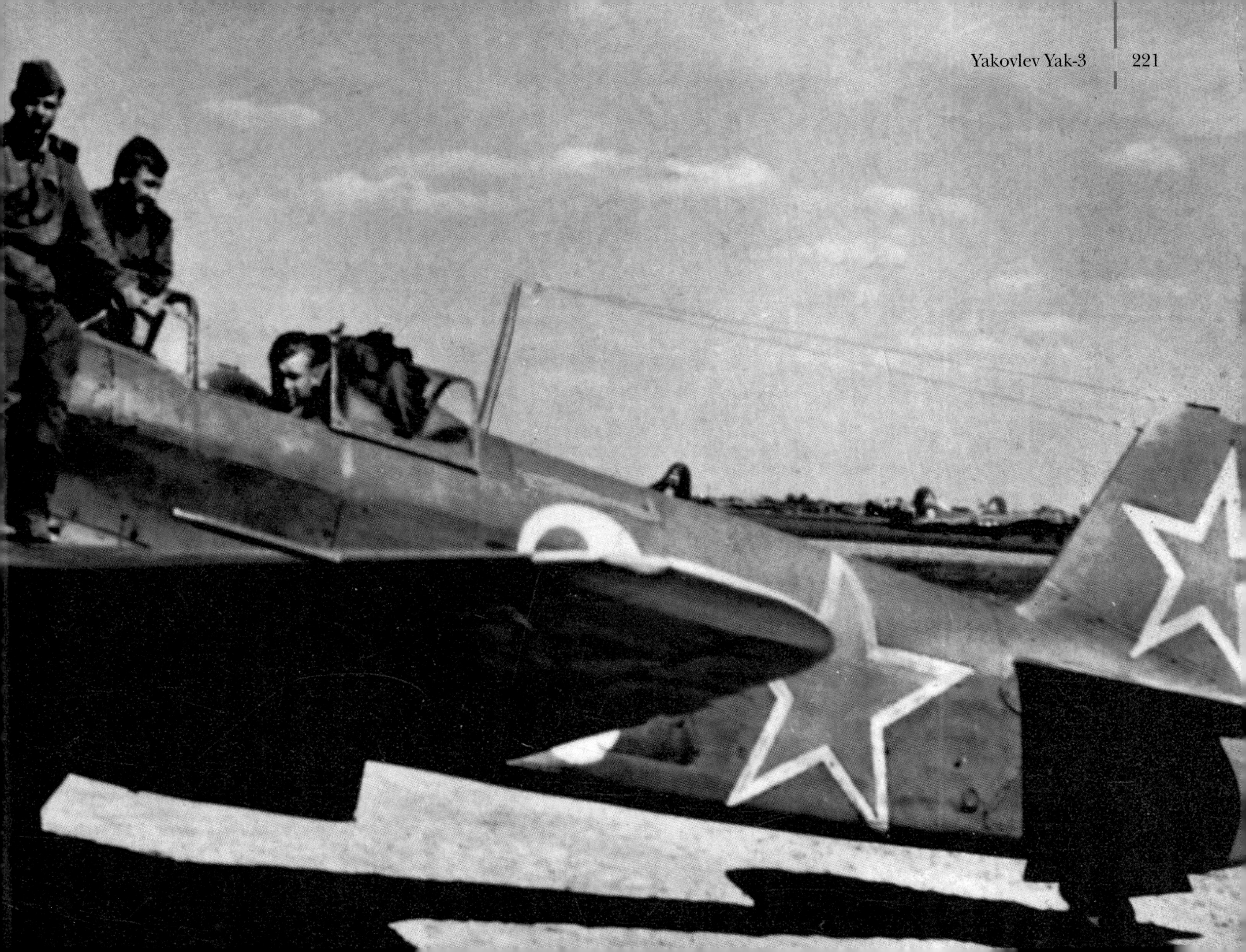

Index

Page numbers in *italics* indicate digital models or photographs.

Picture Credits

All Artworks © Military Visualizations, Inc. (www.milviz.com)

Photographs:
Art-Tech/Aerospace: 16–17, 34–35, 46–47, 82–83, 88–89, 100–101, 106–107, 112–113, 124–125, 142–143, 154–155, 160–161, 166–167, 172–173, 178–179, 184–185, 190–191, 202–203, 220–221

Art-Tech/MARS: 22–23, 28–29, 40–41, 52–53, 58–59, 64–65, 70–71, 76–77, 94–95, 118–119, 130–131, 148–149, 208–209, 214–215

Cody Images: 136–137, 196–197